GUADEI TRAVEL GUIDE

The Updated Guide to the Must-See Attractions, Things to Do, Hotels, Itinerary, Beaches, Culture, Restaurants and Foods to Eat. Everything to Know Before Planning Your Trip

ALEXA MARCUS

Copyright © 2024 by Alexa Marcus

All rights reserved. No part of this publication may be reproduced, distributed, or transmitted in any form or by any means, including photocopying, recording, or other electronic or mechanical methods, without the prior written permission of the publisher.

TABLE OF CONTENTS

INTRODUCTION.. 5
    About Guadeloupe..7
    Reasons to Love Guadeloupe.. 9
    History and Culture Overview.. 11

CHAPTER 1: PLANNING YOUR TRIP TO GUADELOUPE. 13
    When to Visit Guadeloupe.. 15
    How to Get to Guadeloupe... 17
    Getting Around Guadeloupe... 19
    Where to Stay: Neighbourhoods in Guadeloupe.................... 21
    What to Pack... 23
    Entry and Visa Requirements..26
    Currency and Language..28
    Suggested Budget..29
    Money-Saving Tips...31
    Best Places to Book Your Trip.. 34

CHAPTER 2: MUST-SEE ATTRACTIONS AND LANDMARKS.. 37
    Pointe-à-Pitre..39
    La Soufrière Volcano.. 41
    Grande-Anse Beach.. 43
    Fort Napoléon des Saintes.. 45
    Jardin Botanique de Deshaies.. 47
    Plage de la Perle... 49
    Memorial ACTe...51
    Carbet Falls.. 53
    Les Saintes..55
    Guadeloupe National Park... 57
    La Grande Vigie..59

Anse du Souffleur... 61
CHAPTER 3: ACCOMMODATION OPTIONS................ 63
Best Luxury Hotels and Resorts|..65
Budget-Friendly Accommodations..67
Unique Stays and Local Favorites.. 69
Practical Tips for Booking Accommodations.......................71
CHAPTER 4: DINING AND CUISINE......................... 74
Marché de Sainte-Anne: A Culinary Adventure....................76
Le Ti'Punch Bar: Sipping Island Elixirs................................. 78
Best Restaurants and Eateries... 80
Local Flavors and Must-Try Dishes....................................... 82
Dining Etiquette.. 84
CHAPTER 5: THINGS TO DO AND OUTDOOR ACTIVITIES..86
Hiking La Soufrière: Trails and Thrills................................ 88
Water Adventures: Diving, Snorkeling, and More................90
Exploring Les Saintes Islands: Beyond the Horizon.............92
Beach Activities: Relaxation and Recreation........................ 94
CHAPTER 6: ART, CULTURE AND ENTERTAINMENT 96
Local Arts and Crafts.. 98
Museums and Galleries.. 100
Festivals and Events..102
Nightlife and Entertainment.. 104
Local Markets, Shopping, and Souvenirs............................ 106
CHAPTER 7: 7-DAY ITINERARY IN GUADELOUPE.. 108
Day 1: A Warm Guadeloupean Welcome............................ 108
Day 2: Basse-Terre's Natural Wonders............................... 109
Day 3: Les Saintes Archipelago Expedition........................ 110
Day 4: Guadeloupe National Park Adventure.....................110
Day 5: Cultural Exploration in Saint-François.................... 111
Day 6: Culinary Delights in Sainte-Anne............................ 112

Day 7: Farewell to Guadeloupe..113
CHAPTER 8: PRACTICAL INFORMATION AND TIPS 114
Etiquette and Customs.. 114
Language and Communication..117
Simple French Phrases to Know...119
Health and Safety Tips for Your Guadeloupe Adventure..... 121
Emergency Contacts..124
Communication and Internet Access in Guadeloupe...........126
Useful Apps, Websites, and Maps..129
CONCLUSION..131

INTRODUCTION

Nestled in the heart of the Caribbean, my journey to Guadeloupe was more than just a vacation; it was a soul-stirring experience painted in hues of turquoise seas and emerald landscapes. The moment I set foot on this tropical haven, I felt the warm embrace of a place that transcends the ordinary.

As I landed at Pointe-à-Pitre International Airport, the air was laced with the scent of blooming flowers, a fragrant welcome to paradise. The vibrant colors of the island greeted me, setting the stage for an unforgettable adventure.

One of the highlights of my journey was the trek up La Soufrière Volcano. The trail, flanked by lush greenery, led to a summit that unveiled panoramic views of the island. The air was crisp, and the sight of the crater left me in awe – a reminder of nature's raw power.

The silky sands of Grande Anse Beach provided the perfect canvas for relaxation. With each gentle wave, I felt the stress of everyday life wash away. The sun painted the sky in hues of orange and pink as I savored the simplicity of a perfect sunset.

A short ferry ride transported me to the enchanting Les Saintes Islands. Terre-de-Haut, with its charming streets and friendly locals, felt like a step back in time. I explored quaint shops, indulged in local delicacies, and found solace in the unhurried pace of island life.

My choice to stay at Habitation Grande Anse proved to be a stroke of genius. The bungalows, nestled in nature's embrace, provided a sense of tranquility that echoed the island's spirit.

Waking up to the sounds of birds and the rustle of palm leaves was a daily gift.

The Marché de Sainte-Anne became my culinary playground, where exotic fruits and spices beckoned. The Le Ti'Punch Bar, with its laid-back vibe and signature cocktails, became my evening haven, where each sip was a toast to the island's rich flavors.

Guadeloupe's culture unfolded before me in a dance of rhythms and colors. From Creole heritage to vibrant festivals, every moment was an immersion into the island's soul. Museums and galleries became windows into the rich tapestry of Guadeloupean art and history.

As I bid farewell to this Caribbean gem, I carried with me not just memories but a profound connection to a place that felt like a home away from home. Guadeloupe is not just an island; it's an emotion, a melody, and a piece of paradise etched in my heart.

Are you ready to create your own memories in Guadeloupe? Dive into the pages of this guide, let the colors of the island guide you, and embark on a journey that promises not just a vacation but a transformative experience. Your adventure awaits – click Buy Now and let the magic begin.

About Guadeloupe

Guadeloupe, a French-Caribbean archipelago, is not just a destination; it's an immersive experience where every corner tells a unique story. Nestled in the Lesser Antilles, this tropical haven is a harmonious blend of French sophistication and Caribbean charm. As you explore this island gem, you'll find yourself enchanted by its diverse landscapes, each more captivating than the last.

The island's heartbeat, Pointe-à-Pitre, is a vibrant city where modernity intertwines with rich history. Stroll through its bustling markets, such as the lively Spice Market, where the air is filled with the aroma of exotic spices and local delicacies. Beyond the urban pulse, Guadeloupe unfolds as a haven for nature enthusiasts, with Basse-Terre National Park boasting not just the iconic La Soufrière Volcano but also lush rainforests and cascading waterfalls that paint the landscape in hues of green.

Guadeloupe's cultural tapestry is woven with influences from Africa, Europe, and the Caribbean, creating a unique Creole identity. This rich cultural blend is palpable in the vibrant festivals that color the island throughout the year, each celebration a testament to the islanders' love for life and community.

The archipelago's cuisine is a culinary journey that tantalizes the taste buds. From the fresh catch of the day at the bustling fish markets to the street-side stalls offering spicy bokits (sandwiches), Guadeloupean cuisine is a symphony of flavors. The local markets, such as the Sainte-Anne Market, provide a sensory feast where tropical fruits and spices take center stage.

For those seeking relaxation, the pristine beaches beckon. Beyond the renowned Grande Anse, you'll discover hidden coves and secluded shores, each offering a slice of paradise. The underwater world is equally mesmerizing, with coral reefs teeming with marine life, inviting snorkelers and divers to explore the vibrant aquatic ecosystems.

Guadeloupe is not just an escape; it's an invitation to a slower pace of life, where the rhythm of the islands guides your journey. From the charming architecture of colonial buildings to the lively beats of Gwo Ka music, the island embraces you with open arms. Whether you're navigating the winding streets of Pointe-à-Pitre or meandering through the historic sites, Guadeloupe is a captivating canvas waiting for your unique imprint.

This French-Caribbean gem is more than a destination; it's an emotion, a melody, and an everlasting memory etched in the hearts of those fortunate enough to experience its magic. Prepare to be captivated, enchanted, and forever changed by the allure of Guadeloupe – a piece of paradise that transcends the ordinary.

Reasons to Love Guadeloupe

Guadeloupe, with its captivating blend of Caribbean warmth and French sophistication, is a destination that steals hearts and leaves an indelible mark on every traveler. Here are compelling reasons why falling in love with Guadeloupe is not just inevitable but utterly delightful.

1. Breathtaking Diversity: Guadeloupe isn't just an island; it's an archipelago of wonders. From the volcanic landscapes of Basse-Terre to the coral-fringed beaches of Grande-Terre, each corner presents a different facet of natural beauty. The variety is not just scenic; it's a testament to the island's rich ecological diversity.

2. Creole Culture and Heritage: The heartbeat of Guadeloupe resonates with the rhythms of Creole culture. From the infectious beats of Gwo Ka music to the vibrant festivals that color the streets, the island celebrates its unique heritage with pride. Every step is a dance, and every smile is a testament to the warmth of its people.

3. Culinary Symphony: Guadeloupean cuisine is a love letter to the senses. Fresh seafood, tropical fruits, and an array of spices create a culinary symphony that leaves taste buds tingling. Indulge in local specialties like accras and colombo, and don't forget to sip on the island's signature Ti'Punch cocktail.

4. Hidden Beach Paradises: While Grande Anse is a well-known beauty, Guadeloupe hides secret beaches like treasures waiting to be discovered. From the secluded coves of Îlet du Gosier to the pristine shores of Plage de la Caravelle, each beach is a private haven for relaxation and rejuvenation.

5. Les Saintes Islands Magic: A short ferry ride transports you to the enchanting Les Saintes Islands. Terre-de-Haut, with its pastel-colored houses and welcoming locals, feels like a step into a Caribbean fairy tale. The magic of these islands is not just in the scenery but in the unhurried pace of life.

6. Adventure Awaits: Whether you're hiking up the trails of La Soufrière or exploring the underwater wonders of the Pigeon Islands, Guadeloupe is an adventure playground. The thrill of outdoor activities is complemented by the sheer beauty of the natural surroundings.

7. Romantic Retreats: Guadeloupe sets the stage for romance like no other. Intimate stays like Habitation Grande Anse offer a tranquil escape, where the rustle of palm leaves becomes a love song. The sunsets, the moonlit beaches, and the serenity make it an ideal destination for couples.

8. Welcoming Locals: The people of Guadeloupe embody the true spirit of hospitality. Locals welcome visitors with open arms, eager to share their culture and make every traveler feel like a part of the island family. The genuine warmth adds an extra layer of charm to the entire experience.

In Guadeloupe, love isn't just in the air; it's in the landscapes, the flavors, and the culture. It's an affair that begins with the first glimpse of turquoise waters and continues with every beat of the island's heart. Discover the reasons to love Guadeloupe – a place where every moment is a celebration of life, love, and the sheer joy of being in paradise.

History and Culture Overview

Guadeloupe's history is a captivating tapestry woven with threads of indigenous heritage, colonial legacies, and a vibrant Creole culture. Long before European explorers set foot on these shores, the Arawak and Carib peoples inhabited the islands. Christopher Columbus, during his second voyage in 1493, claimed Guadeloupe for Spain, but it wasn't until the 17th century that French settlers established a permanent presence.

Colonial struggles ensued as the islands passed between French and British hands multiple times, shaping the cultural landscape. The blending of African, European, and indigenous influences during this period laid the foundation for Guadeloupe's unique Creole identity. The remnants of this colonial history are visible in the architecture of Pointe-à-Pitre, where colonial buildings stand as silent witnesses to a bygone era.

The 19th century saw the abolition of slavery, a pivotal moment that left an indelible mark on the social fabric. The island's cultural richness owes much to the resilience of the Afro-Caribbean population, who, despite the harsh legacy of slavery, infused the region with their traditions, music, and vibrant celebrations.

In more recent history, Guadeloupe became an Overseas Department of France in 1946, solidifying its ties with the European nation. The French influence is evident in everyday life, from the language spoken to the legal and educational systems. This duality, being both Caribbean and distinctly French, is a defining feature of Guadeloupe's contemporary identity.

Culturally, Guadeloupe is a melting pot where traditions are celebrated with fervor. The beats of Gwo Ka music echo the island's African roots, and traditional dances like the Quadrille pay homage to European influences. Festivals, such as Carnival and the Fête de la Musique, bring the community together in joyous celebration, showcasing the vibrant colors and rhythms that define Guadeloupean culture.

The island's commitment to preserving its cultural heritage is evident in its museums and galleries. The Memorial ACTe in Pointe-à-Pitre stands as a powerful testament to the history of slavery, providing a poignant and educational experience. Artistic expressions, from paintings to sculptures, offer a deeper understanding of the complexities that have shaped the Guadeloupean narrative.

Guadeloupe's history and culture are not just chapters in a book; they are a living, breathing essence that colors every aspect of island life. It's a journey through time, where echoes of the past harmonize with the rhythms of the present, creating a cultural symphony that invites visitors to become a part of the island's rich narrative.

CHAPTER 1: PLANNING YOUR TRIP TO GUADELOUPE

Embarking on a journey to Guadeloupe is a thrilling venture, and careful planning ensures a seamless escape into this Caribbean paradise. Determining when to visit is the initial key, as the archipelago enjoys a tropical climate, with the dry season from December to May offering ideal weather for exploration. Once your timing is set, navigating how to get to Guadeloupe becomes paramount. Pointe-à-Pitre International Airport serves as the primary gateway, welcoming international flights that connect travelers to this idyllic destination.

Getting around Guadeloupe involves uncovering the diverse landscapes of both Basse-Terre and Grande-Terre islands. Whether it's exploring the volcanic trails of La Soufrière or the pristine beaches of Grande Anse, having a reliable mode of transportation is essential. Neighborhoods in Guadeloupe vary in character, from the bustling hub of Pointe-à-Pitre to the serene retreats in Sainte-Anne or Deshaies, offering distinct experiences to suit every traveler's preferences.

Packing for Guadeloupe is an art, with essentials ranging from lightweight clothing for the warm climate to sturdy footwear for island exploration. Understanding entry and visa requirements is crucial, and a valid passport is your ticket to the tropical haven. In terms of currency, the Euro is the official tender, and French is widely spoken, providing a glimpse into the island's European ties.

Crafting a suggested budget ensures that your Guadeloupean adventure aligns with your financial plans. Consider money-saving tips, such as exploring local markets for budget-friendly meals and utilizing public transportation for cost-effective travel. To kickstart your journey, finding the best places to book your trip involves navigating reputable platforms that offer a range of accommodation, flight, and activity options. As you delve into the planning phase, remember that each element is a thread weaving into the vibrant tapestry of your Guadeloupean escapade.

When to Visit Guadeloupe

Choosing the right time to visit Guadeloupe is a crucial step in ensuring a memorable and enjoyable experience. The archipelago enjoys a tropical climate with two distinct seasons: the dry season and the wet season.

Dry Season (December to May):
The dry season, spanning from December to May, is considered the best time to visit Guadeloupe. During these months, the weather is generally sunny, and rainfall is minimal. The temperatures hover around 75°F to 89°F (24°C to 32°C), creating perfect conditions for beach days, outdoor activities, and exploration. This period also aligns with the peak tourist season, especially around Christmas and New Year, so early bookings for accommodations and activities are advisable.

Wet Season (June to November):
The wet season, from June to November, brings higher humidity and increased chances of rainfall, with the peak of the hurricane season occurring from August to October. While this period may see occasional heavy rains, it also offers lush green landscapes and fewer crowds. Travelers willing to embrace some rain showers can benefit from lower accommodation prices and a quieter atmosphere. However, it's essential to stay updated on weather forecasts and potential tropical storms during these months.

Special Considerations:
Keep in mind that Guadeloupe's climate can vary between the islands of Basse-Terre and Grande-Terre. Basse-Terre, with its mountainous terrain, tends to receive more rainfall, leading to a

lusher landscape. Grande-Terre, on the other hand, is flatter and generally drier.

Overall, the ideal time to visit ultimately depends on your personal preferences. If you crave sun-drenched days for beach activities and outdoor adventures, the dry season is ideal. However, if you appreciate a quieter atmosphere, lower prices, and don't mind occasional rain, the wet season may offer a unique and more budget-friendly experience.

How to Get to Guadeloupe

Getting to Guadeloupe is an exciting journey, and the primary gateway is Pointe-à-Pitre International Airport (PTP). Several international airlines operate direct flights to Guadeloupe, connecting the archipelago to major cities in Europe, North America, and the Caribbean.

International Flights:
From Europe, airlines such as Air France, Corsair, and Level provide direct flights to Guadeloupe. Departing from North America, American Airlines, Air Canada, and Norwegian Air Shuttle offer convenient options for travelers. The flight duration varies depending on your departure location but typically ranges from 4 to 9 hours.

Connecting Flights:
For those without direct flight options, connecting flights through nearby hubs such as Paris, Miami, or San Juan are common. Connecting flights may extend the travel time but can offer flexibility in terms of airlines and potential cost savings.

Cruise Ships:
Another enchanting way to reach Guadeloupe is by cruise ship. The Pointe-à-Pitre Cruise Terminal welcomes cruise liners, providing a scenic arrival with views of the bustling city and surrounding landscapes.

Traveling Between the Islands:
Once in Guadeloupe, exploring the different islands is easily done by ferry. Regular ferry services operate between Basse-Terre and Grande-Terre, as well as to the neighboring islands of Les Saintes, Marie-Galante, and La Désirade.

Getting Around the Islands:
Guadeloupe offers various transportation options for island exploration. Renting a car is a popular choice, providing flexibility to discover both Basse-Terre and Grande-Terre at your own pace. Taxis, buses, and organized tours are also available, ensuring convenient access to the archipelago's diverse landscapes and attractions.

Whether arriving by air or sea, the journey to Guadeloupe sets the stage for an unforgettable tropical adventure. The combination of international flights, local ferries, and efficient island transportation options makes reaching and navigating this Caribbean paradise a seamless and enjoyable experience.

Getting Around Guadeloupe

Navigating the captivating landscapes of Guadeloupe is an integral part of the adventure, and the archipelago offers various transportation options for seamless island exploration.

Renting a Car:
One of the most popular and convenient ways to get around Guadeloupe is by renting a car. Car rental agencies are readily available at Pointe-à-Pitre International Airport and other key locations. With well-maintained roads and clear signage, driving allows travelers to explore both Basse-Terre and Grande-Terre at their own pace. It's essential to have a valid driver's license, and driving is on the right side of the road.

Taxis:
Taxis are a reliable mode of transportation, especially for short distances or when exploring without a set itinerary. Taxis can be found at airports, ferry terminals, and in urban areas. While they operate on fixed rates, it's advisable to confirm the fare with the driver before the journey begins.

Buses:
Guadeloupe's public bus system is an affordable option for those looking to navigate the islands economically. Buses connect major towns and cities, providing access to popular attractions. However, schedules may vary, and it's advisable to check timetables in advance.

Ferries:
Exploring the diverse islands of Guadeloupe is easily done by ferry. Regular ferry services operate between Basse-Terre and Grande-Terre, as well as to the neighboring islands of Les

Saintes, Marie-Galante, and La Désirade. Ferries offer not only transportation but also scenic views of the Caribbean Sea.

Organized Tours:
For a hassle-free experience, organized tours and excursions are available, providing guided exploration of Guadeloupe's natural wonders and cultural attractions. Whether hiking in Basse-Terre's rainforests or snorkeling in the crystal-clear waters, tours offer insight and convenience.

Cycling and Walking:
For the eco-conscious traveler, cycling and walking are delightful ways to explore the local surroundings. Guadeloupe offers a network of hiking trails, especially in Basse-Terre, where you can immerse yourself in the lush landscapes and discover hidden gems.

With a variety of transportation options, getting around Guadeloupe is not just a means to an end; it's an integral part of the adventure. Whether you choose the flexibility of a rental car, the convenience of taxis, or the scenic routes of ferries, each mode of transportation unveils a different aspect of the island's charm, ensuring a memorable and immersive travel experience.

Where to Stay: Neighbourhoods in Guadeloupe

Guadeloupe offers a diverse array of neighborhoods, each with its own unique character and charm, providing visitors with a range of accommodation options to suit their preferences.

Pointe-à-Pitre:
As the economic and cultural hub of Guadeloupe, Pointe-à-Pitre is a vibrant city with bustling markets, colonial architecture, and a lively atmosphere. Choosing accommodation in the city center offers convenient access to historical sites like Place de la Victoire and local markets such as Spice Market. It's an ideal location for those seeking a blend of urban exploration and cultural immersion.

Sainte-Anne:
For travelers in search of pristine beaches and a more relaxed atmosphere, Sainte-Anne is a popular choice. This coastal town on Grande-Terre boasts postcard-perfect beaches like Plage de la Caravelle and Plage de Bois Jolan. Accommodations range from beachfront resorts to cozy guesthouses, offering a tranquil escape with the sound of waves as your backdrop.

Deshaies:
Nestled on the northwest coast of Basse-Terre, Deshaies is a charming village known for its lush landscapes and tranquil ambiance. Travelers seeking a laid-back retreat will find a variety of accommodations here, from intimate bed and breakfasts to boutique hotels. The nearby Jardin Botanique de Deshaies adds an extra touch of natural beauty to the surroundings.

Le Gosier:
Situated between Pointe-à-Pitre and Sainte-Anne, Le Gosier is a coastal town known for its beaches and vibrant nightlife. The area offers a mix of accommodations, including beachfront resorts and budget-friendly hotels. Travelers can enjoy the convenience of local restaurants, bars, and the lively atmosphere along the waterfront.

Saint-François:
On the southeastern tip of Grande-Terre, Saint-François is a haven for water enthusiasts. With marinas, golf courses, and pristine beaches like Plage des Raisins Clairs, it's an excellent choice for those seeking a more upscale and active vacation. Resorts, villas, and boutique hotels cater to a range of preferences.

Bouillante:
For nature lovers and diving enthusiasts, Bouillante on the western coast of Basse-Terre offers a tranquil setting amidst lush greenery. The area is known for its marine reserve and proximity to the Cousteau Underwater Reserve. Accommodations here range from eco-friendly lodges to charming guesthouses.

Whether you prefer the urban energy of Pointe-à-Pitre, the beachfront bliss of Sainte-Anne, or the nature-infused tranquility of Deshaies, Guadeloupe's diverse neighborhoods ensure that your stay is not just about accommodation but an immersive experience in the heart of the Caribbean.

What to Pack

Preparing for your adventure in Guadeloupe requires thoughtful packing to ensure you're ready for the tropical climate, diverse landscapes, and various activities. Here's a guide on what to pack for a memorable stay in this Caribbean paradise:

1. Lightweight Clothing:
Pack breathable and lightweight clothing suitable for the tropical climate. Think shorts, T-shirts, sundresses, and swimwear. A light jacket or shawl might come in handy for cooler evenings.

2. Sturdy Footwear:
Comfortable and sturdy footwear is essential, especially if you plan on exploring nature trails or taking part in outdoor activities. Pack sandals for the beach and comfortable walking shoes or hiking boots for exploring.

3. Sun Protection:
Guadeloupe is blessed with abundant sunshine. Pack sunscreen with a high SPF, sunglasses, and a wide-brimmed hat to shield yourself from the sun's rays. A reusable water bottle is also crucial to stay hydrated.

4. Insect Repellent:
Given the tropical setting, insect repellent is a must, especially if you plan on exploring nature reserves or spending time outdoors. Consider packing a travel-sized bottle for convenience.

5. Snorkeling Gear:
If you're a fan of underwater exploration, bring your own snorkeling gear. While some accommodations and tour operators

may provide equipment, having your own ensures a comfortable fit.

6. Daypack:
A small daypack is handy for day trips, hikes, and beach outings. It can carry essentials like water, sunscreen, a hat, a camera, and any souvenirs you may pick up along the way.

7. Lightweight Towel:
Pack a compact and quick-drying towel for beach days and water activities. Some accommodations may provide towels, but having your own is convenient for impromptu beach visits.

8. Waterproof Phone Case:
Protect your electronics from unexpected splashes or rain by bringing a waterproof phone case. This is particularly useful if you plan on taking photos near the water.

9. Travel Adapter:
Guadeloupe, being a French overseas department, uses European-style electrical outlets. Ensure you pack a travel adapter to charge your devices.

10. First Aid Kit:
A basic first aid kit with essentials like bandages, pain relievers, motion sickness medication, and any personal medications you may need is advisable for unforeseen situations.

11. French Phrasebook:
While English is spoken in tourist areas, having a basic French phrasebook can be helpful and appreciated by locals. Learning a few common phrases adds a personal touch to your interactions.

12. Eco-Friendly Products:
Consider bringing reusable items like a water bottle, shopping bag, and utensils to minimize environmental impact during your travels.

By packing smartly and considering the specific needs of a tropical destination, you'll be well-prepared to make the most of your time in Guadeloupe.

Entry and Visa Requirements

Guadeloupe, as an overseas department of France, follows the entry and visa requirements set by France for travelers. Here's an overview to help you plan your visit:

1. Visa Requirements:
For citizens of many countries, a visa is not required for short stays of up to 90 days within a 180-day period for tourism, business, or family visits. However, specific requirements can vary based on your nationality, so it's essential to check the visa regulations for your country on the official website of the French government or consult with the French embassy or consulate.

2. Passport Validity:
Ensure your passport is valid for at least three months beyond your planned departure date from Guadeloupe. It's advisable to have a buffer period to avoid any unforeseen issues.

3. Schengen Area Rules:
Guadeloupe is part of the Schengen Area, which allows for border-free travel across participating European countries. If you plan to visit other Schengen countries during your trip, your time in Guadeloupe counts towards the 90-day limit within a 180-day period.

4. Extension of Stay:
If you wish to extend your stay beyond the initial 90 days, you must contact the local prefecture (government office) in Guadeloupe before your authorized stay expires. Extensions are granted based on specific circumstances, such as family reunification or other valid reasons.

5. Proof of Onward Travel:
While not always strictly enforced, it's advisable to have proof of onward travel when arriving in Guadeloupe. This could be a return ticket or proof of travel to another destination.

6. Yellow Fever Vaccination:
Guadeloupe does not require a yellow fever vaccination for entry unless you are arriving from a country with a risk of yellow fever transmission. In such cases, a valid yellow fever vaccination certificate may be required.

Before your trip, consider reaching out to the French embassy or consulate in your country for personalized assistance based on your specific circumstances.

Currency and Language

Guadeloupe uses the Euro (EUR) as its official currency, as it is an Overseas Department of France. It's advisable to have some cash on hand for small purchases and transactions, especially in more remote areas. Credit cards are widely accepted in hotels, restaurants, and larger establishments, but it's a good idea to check for acceptance before making purchases.

French is the official language of Guadeloupe, reflecting its status as a French overseas department. While French is the primary language spoken, many locals, especially in the tourism industry, may also speak English. However, it's helpful to know some basic French phrases, as this can enhance your overall experience and interactions with locals, particularly in more traditional or rural areas where English may be less commonly spoken.

In addition to French and English, Guadeloupe is influenced by Creole culture, and Guadeloupean Creole (Créole Guadeloupéen) is spoken by some residents. While not essential for visitors to speak Creole, locals may appreciate any effort to learn and use a few basic Creole expressions.

Overall, language should not pose a significant barrier for travelers, especially in tourist areas, but having a basic understanding of French can enhance communication and cultural exchange.

Suggested Budget

Creating a budget for your trip to Guadeloupe depends on various factors, including your travel style, preferences, and planned activities. Guadeloupe, being a French overseas department, has a cost of living that may be higher than some other Caribbean destinations. Here's a general breakdown of expenses to help you plan your budget:

Accommodation:
Accommodation costs can vary based on the type of lodging you choose. Budget travelers can find guesthouses and hostels, while mid-range options include hotels and vacation rentals. Upscale resorts and boutique hotels are available for those seeking a more luxurious stay.
Budget: €40-80 per night
Mid-Range: €80-150 per night
Luxury: €150 and above per night

Meals:
Dining costs can vary depending on where you eat. Local markets and street food stalls offer budget-friendly options, while restaurants and beachfront cafes may be slightly more expensive.
Budget: €10-20 per meal
Mid-Range: €20-50 per meal
Luxury: €50 and above per meal

Transportation:
Renting a car provides flexibility for exploring the islands, but it comes with costs like fuel and rental fees. Public buses are more economical, and taxis are available for shorter distances.
Car Rental: €40-80 per day
Public Bus: €1-2 per ride

Taxi: €10-20 for short distances

Activities and Excursions:
Guadeloupe offers a range of activities, from hiking in national parks to snorkeling in coral reefs. Entrance fees to attractions and guided tours contribute to this part of the budget.
National Park Entrance: €5-15
Boat Tours or Excursions: €50 and above

Miscellaneous:
Include miscellaneous expenses such as shopping, souvenirs, and any additional activities or attractions not covered in the categories above.

Overall Daily Budget:
Budget Traveler: €70-150 per day
Mid-Range Traveler: €150-300 per day
Luxury Traveler: €300 and above per day

These are general estimates and can vary based on individual choices. Additionally, it's important to factor in any specific activities or experiences you plan to include in your itinerary. Always consider extra funds for unexpected expenses and emergencies. Keep in mind that these estimates are in Euros (EUR), and currency exchange rates may influence your actual expenses if your home currency is different.

Money-Saving Tips

Exploring Guadeloupe on a budget is not only feasible but can enhance your travel experience by immersing you in local culture and natural beauty. Here are some money-saving tips to make the most of your trip without breaking the bank:

1. Local Markets and Grocery Stores:
Opt for fresh produce, local snacks, and ingredients from markets and grocery stores. This not only allows you to experience local flavors but can also be more budget-friendly than dining out for every meal.

2. Public Transportation:
Utilize the public bus system for affordable transportation between towns and cities. It's a cost-effective way to explore the islands. If you're in a group, consider sharing a taxi for short distances to split the fare.

3. Accommodation Choices:
Explore a variety of accommodation options, from guesthouses to vacation rentals. Booking accommodations away from major tourist areas may offer more budget-friendly rates. Consider staying in self-catering accommodations with kitchen facilities to save on dining expenses.

4. Picnic on the Beach:
Pack a picnic and enjoy a meal on one of Guadeloupe's beautiful beaches. Local markets provide fresh fruits, baguettes, and cheeses for a delightful beachfront experience without the restaurant prices.

5. Free and Low-Cost Activities:
Take advantage of the many free or low-cost activities Guadeloupe has to offer, such as hiking trails in the national parks, exploring local markets, or relaxing on the beaches. Nature reserves and botanical gardens often have nominal entrance fees.

6. Water Activities:
Bring your snorkeling gear to explore coral reefs and marine life without the cost of renting equipment. Many beaches offer excellent snorkeling opportunities. Additionally, public beaches are often free or have a nominal entrance fee.

7. Explore Les Saintes Independently:
Instead of booking guided tours to Les Saintes Islands, consider exploring independently. Ferries operate regularly from the mainland, allowing you to create your own itinerary and potentially save on tour costs.

8. Travel Off-Peak:
Consider traveling during the shoulder seasons, avoiding peak tourist times. Accommodation prices may be lower, and you'll experience a quieter atmosphere at popular attractions.

9. BYOB (Bring Your Own Bottle):
Bring a reusable water bottle and refill it throughout your trip. This not only reduces single-use plastic but also saves money compared to buying bottled water.

10. Learn Basic French Phrases:
Knowing a few basic French phrases can be advantageous when interacting with locals. In some cases, it might lead to better deals or recommendations.

By incorporating these money-saving tips, you can enjoy the beauty and culture of Guadeloupe while keeping your travel budget in check. Embracing local experiences and savoring the natural wonders of the islands can be both enriching and cost-effective.

Best Places to Book Your Trip

Finding the best places to book your trip to Guadeloupe involves exploring various online platforms and travel agencies that offer comprehensive options for accommodations, flights, and activities. Here are some popular and reliable platforms to consider:

1. Booking.com:
Booking.com is known for its extensive range of accommodation options, from hotels and resorts to guesthouses and vacation rentals. The platform provides user reviews, flexible booking options, and often offers competitive prices.

2. Airbnb:
For a more personalized and local experience, consider Airbnb. You can find unique stays such as private homes, apartments, or even rooms in local residences. It's an excellent option for those seeking a home-like atmosphere.

3. Expedia:
Expedia is a complete travel platform that allows you to book flights, accommodations, and car rentals in one place. The website often features package deals, allowing you to save on your overall travel expenses.

4. Travel Agencies:
Traditional travel agencies or online agencies like Travelocity or CheapTickets can provide package deals and discounts on flights and accommodations. It's worth comparing prices on multiple platforms to find the best deals.

5. Google Flights:
Google Flights is a powerful tool for finding and comparing flight prices. It allows you to explore different dates, airlines, and routes to find the most cost-effective options for your journey to Guadeloupe.

6. Skyscanner:
Skyscanner is a popular flight search engine that can help you find the best deals on airfare. It compares prices from various airlines and online travel agencies to ensure you get the most competitive rates.

7. Local Tour Operators:
Consider reaching out to local tour operators in Guadeloupe for specific activities and excursions. They often provide insight into unique experiences and may offer more personalized services.

8. Hopper:
Hopper is an app that predicts and tracks flight prices, helping you decide the optimal time to book for the best deals. It provides recommendations on when to purchase tickets to get the lowest prices.

9. Agoda:
Agoda specializes in hotel bookings and often features competitive rates, particularly in the Asia-Pacific region. It's worth checking for deals on accommodations in Guadeloupe.

10. Official Tourism Websites:
Visit the official tourism websites of Guadeloupe, which may provide information on local attractions, events, and sometimes even exclusive promotions. These websites can offer valuable insights into planning your trip.

Before finalizing any bookings, always read reviews from other travelers and check the terms and conditions, including cancellation policies. Flexibility in your travel dates and the ability to book accommodation and flights as a package may also result in cost savings.

CHAPTER 2: MUST-SEE ATTRACTIONS AND LANDMARKS

Embarking on a journey through Guadeloupe unveils a tapestry of must-see attractions and landmarks that paint a vivid portrait of the archipelago's diverse beauty. Begin your exploration in Pointe-à-Pitre, the lively capital, where vibrant markets, colonial architecture, and the lively rhythm of Creole culture converge. As you traverse the city, the essence of Guadeloupean life comes to life, with local vendors beckoning you to discover the flavors of the Spice Market and the historic allure of Place de la Victoire.

Venture beyond the cityscape to encounter the majestic La Soufrière Volcano, an iconic symbol of Guadeloupe's geological wonders. The hike to its summit promises not only panoramic views of the archipelago but also a glimpse into the island's volcanic history. Descending to the coast, Grande-Anse Beach unfolds, a stretch of powdery sand framed by turquoise waters. This idyllic haven invites relaxation, with the gentle lull of waves creating a harmonious symphony beneath the Caribbean sun.

Continue your odyssey to Fort Napoléon des Saintes, a historic fortress perched atop Terre-de-Haut in Les Saintes. The fort's strategic position offers commanding views of the archipelago, providing a fascinating glimpse into the region's maritime history. Jardin Botanique de Deshaies, nestled on Basse-Terre, beckons with lush botanical wonders. Stroll through vibrant flora, from orchids to exotic palms, creating a sensory escape amidst the island's natural abundance.

Plage de la Perle, with its serene shores and crystal-clear waters, invites tranquility, while the Memorial ACTe in Pointe-à-Pitre stands as a poignant tribute to the complex history of slavery in the Caribbean. Carbet Falls, a cascading masterpiece in the heart of Guadeloupe National Park, showcases the island's verdant landscapes, drawing nature enthusiasts to its enchanting embrace. Les Saintes, an archipelago within an archipelago, invites exploration with its pristine bays and charming villages, epitomizing the Caribbean's serene allure.

Embark on a journey to La Grande Vigie, a northern vantage point that unveils panoramic views of the Atlantic, offering a contrast to the Caribbean's calm embrace. Anse du Souffleur, with its golden sands and gentle trade winds, encapsulates the essence of Guadeloupe's coastal serenity. As you traverse these must-see landmarks, each unveils a unique chapter in Guadeloupe's narrative, a testament to the island's natural splendor and rich cultural tapestry.

Pointe-à-Pitre

Nestled on the southwestern coast of Grande-Terre, Pointe-à-Pitre stands as the vibrant beating heart of Guadeloupe. This bustling city, with its colorful markets, colonial architecture, and lively Creole spirit, offers a captivating blend of history, culture, and commerce. The city's central location serves as a gateway for both international travelers and those exploring the wider Guadeloupe archipelago.

Pointe-à-Pitre is accessible primarily through Pointe-à-Pitre International Airport (PTP), situated a short distance from the city center. The airport welcomes flights from major international destinations, ensuring convenient access to this lively hub. Additionally, ferry services connect Pointe-à-Pitre to neighboring islands, facilitating seamless exploration for those eager to venture beyond Grande-Terre.

As you navigate the city's charming streets, Place de la Victoire emerges as a historical centerpiece, surrounded by colonial buildings and showcasing a vibrant local atmosphere. The Spice Market, known locally as Marché aux Épices, beckons with an array of exotic spices, fresh produce, and handmade crafts. Immerse yourself in the lively rhythm of Creole life as you stroll through the market, engaging with local vendors and savoring the diverse flavors of Guadeloupean cuisine.

For those with an appreciation for history, the Schoelcher Museum provides insight into the island's past, with exhibits dedicated to abolitionist Victor Schoelcher and the history of slavery in the Caribbean. Pointe-à-Pitre is also home to the Memorial ACTe, a poignant museum addressing the complex legacy of slavery in the region. The museum stands as a powerful testament to Guadeloupe's commitment to preserving and sharing its cultural heritage.

As evening descends, the city's waterfront comes alive with a vibrant nightlife. Local bars and waterfront cafes offer a perfect setting to unwind, enjoy live music, and savor traditional Caribbean cocktails. Pointe-à-Pitre, with its blend of historical charm and contemporary energy, provides a dynamic introduction to the diverse experiences awaiting travelers in Guadeloupe.

La Soufrière Volcano

Standing as a majestic centerpiece on the island of Basse-Terre, La Soufrière Volcano is a geological marvel and an iconic symbol of Guadeloupe. This active stratovolcano, also known as "La Grande Soufrière," is the highest peak in the Lesser Antilles, rising 1,467 meters (4,813 feet) above sea level. Its commanding presence not only shapes the island's landscape but also offers intrepid travelers a captivating adventure.

Reaching the summit of La Soufrière is a rewarding experience for those seeking both natural beauty and a touch of adventure. The hike to the volcano's summit takes approximately two to three hours, leading through lush rainforests, rocky terrains, and sulfuric landscapes. As you ascend, the trail unveils panoramic vistas of the surrounding Caribbean Sea and the neighboring islands, providing a breathtaking backdrop to the journey.

The allure of La Soufrière lies not only in its geological significance but also in the volcanic activity that shapes its character. At the summit, visitors encounter the crater, where fumaroles release steam, and the unmistakable scent of sulfur fills the air. The sulfur springs add an otherworldly dimension to the landscape, creating an environment that feels both ancient and alive.

Accessing La Soufrière is facilitated by well-maintained hiking trails, and guided tours are available for those seeking expert insight into the volcano's geology and history. It's essential to check the trail conditions and weather before embarking on the hike, as the summit experience may be affected by varying factors.

For nature enthusiasts and adventure seekers, La Soufrière Volcano presents an opportunity to connect with Guadeloupe's geological wonders and immerse themselves in the island's rich natural tapestry. The journey to the summit not only offers a sense of accomplishment but also provides a deeper appreciation for the forces that have shaped this Caribbean jewel.

Grande-Anse Beach

Nestled along the southwestern coast of Basse-Terre, Grande-Anse Beach stands as a picturesque haven of pristine beauty, inviting visitors to bask in the sun and surrender to the tranquility of the Caribbean Sea. Renowned for its expansive stretch of powdery white sand and azure waters, Grande-Anse is a postcard-perfect destination that epitomizes the idyllic allure of Guadeloupe's coastline.

This exquisite beach is easily accessible, located near the town of Deshaies and framed by lush, green hillsides. Its accessibility makes it a popular choice for both locals and tourists seeking a serene escape. Whether you're an avid beachcomber, a sunseeker, or someone yearning for a leisurely stroll along the water's edge, Grande-Anse caters to a spectrum of tropical desires.

The gently curving shoreline of Grande-Anse is a testament to nature's artistry, where the Caribbean waves lap against the shore with a soothing rhythm. The beach's wide expanse provides ample space for relaxation, be it lounging under the shade of coconut palms, engaging in a game of beach volleyball, or simply reveling in the warmth of the sun.

Snorkeling enthusiasts will discover a vibrant underwater world teeming with marine life, as the crystal-clear waters of Grande-Anse offer excellent visibility. The coral reefs near the shoreline provide a kaleidoscopic display of tropical fish, creating an underwater paradise for those eager to explore the depths.

Adjacent to the beach, the small town of Deshaies offers quaint cafes and local eateries, allowing visitors to savor authentic Guadeloupean cuisine. From freshly caught seafood to tropical fruit delights, the culinary offerings complement the beach experience, creating a holistic immersion into the island's culture.

Whether you're seeking solitude, adventure, or simply a sun-drenched day by the sea, Grande-Anse Beach encapsulates the essence of Guadeloupe's coastal allure. It's a place where the harmony of nature and the tranquility of the Caribbean converge, inviting you to unwind and create cherished memories along the shores of this tropical paradise.

Fort Napoléon des Saintes

Perched atop the verdant hills of Terre-de-Haut in Les Saintes, Fort Napoléon stands as a historic sentinel, offering not only panoramic views of the Caribbean Sea but also a captivating journey through time. This well-preserved fortress is a testament to the island's strategic importance and its storied past, inviting visitors to explore its bastions and embrace the charm of Les Saintes.

Constructed in the 19th century, Fort Napoléon was initially built as a defensive fortification during the Napoleonic era. Today, it serves as a museum, providing insight into the history of Les Saintes and the archipelago's maritime significance. The fort's architecture, with its imposing walls and red-roofed buildings, reflects a blend of military precision and Caribbean charm.

The museum within Fort Napoléon showcases a diverse collection of exhibits, including historical artifacts, maritime memorabilia, and insights into the island's colonial past. Visitors can wander through the museum's rooms, each offering a glimpse into different aspects of Les Saintes' cultural and natural heritage. The well-manicured gardens surrounding the fort add to the ambiance, providing a serene backdrop for exploration.

As you traverse the fortress, you'll encounter cannons strategically positioned to overlook the turquoise waters that stretch beyond the coastline. The elevated vantage points offer breathtaking views of the neighboring islands, making Fort Napoléon not just a historical gem but also a scenic destination that captivates the senses.

Access to Fort Napoléon is facilitated by walking trails, allowing visitors to enjoy a leisurely ascent to the summit while soaking in the surrounding landscapes. The journey itself becomes an integral part of the experience, immersing travelers in the natural beauty that Les Saintes has to offer.

Fort Napoléon des Saintes is not just a relic of the past; it's a living testament to the resilience and cultural richness of Les Saintes. The fort's strategic perch, combined with its role as a museum, makes it a must-visit destination for those seeking a blend of history, panoramic views, and the unique charm of this Caribbean archipelago.

Jardin Botanique de Deshaies

Nestled on the lush slopes of Basse-Terre, the Jardin Botanique de Deshaies invites visitors into a botanical paradise where the vibrant colors and fragrances of tropical flora take center stage. This botanical garden, located near the town of Deshaies, unfolds as a sensory tapestry, immersing guests in the rich biodiversity of Guadeloupe while providing a tranquil escape into nature.

Spread across 7 acres, the Jardin Botanique de Deshaies is a haven for plant enthusiasts and those seeking a serene retreat. The garden was designed by the well-known comedian and horticulturist Michel Gaillard, who envisioned a harmonious space where exotic plants, flowers, and trees coexist in perfect synergy. The result is a captivating landscape that showcases the beauty of Caribbean and tropical plant species.

Wandering through the garden's meandering pathways, visitors encounter a diverse collection of flora, from vibrant orchids and bromeliads to towering palms and bamboo groves. The garden's layout allows for a leisurely exploration, with surprises awaiting around every corner. Tropical birds and butterflies flit among the blossoms, adding to the enchanting atmosphere.

One of the highlights of the Jardin Botanique de Deshaies is the on-site animal park, where visitors can encounter a variety of species, including birds, capybaras, and agoutis. This unique feature adds an extra layer of fascination to the overall experience, creating a holistic encounter with nature.

The garden also includes a pond with water lilies and aquatic plants, providing a tranquil setting for reflection. Benches strategically placed throughout the grounds offer visitors the opportunity to pause, absorb the surroundings, and appreciate the serenity of this botanical oasis.

Adjacent to the garden, a café provides a charming spot to relax and enjoy refreshments amidst the greenery. The Jardin Botanique de Deshaies is not only a showcase of botanical wonders but also a testament to the passion for nature that inspired its creation, making it a must-visit destination for those seeking a respite in the heart of Guadeloupe's natural beauty.

Plage de la Perle

Tucked away on the western coast of Basse-Terre, Plage de la Perle emerges as a hidden gem along the shores of Guadeloupe. This pristine beach, aptly named "Pearl Beach," beckons travelers seeking a tranquil haven away from the bustling crowds. With its golden sands, swaying palms, and crystal-clear waters, Plage de la Perle captivates visitors with its unspoiled beauty.

The beach is easily accessible, making it an ideal destination for a day of relaxation or a leisurely afternoon escape. Nestled between Deshaies and Sainte-Rose, Plage de la Perle welcomes those who seek a serene and uncrowded coastal retreat. For beachgoers trying to relax, the tranquil Caribbean waves gently lap against the shore, providing a calming sound.

Surrounded by lush greenery, Plage de la Perle offers a sense of seclusion, providing the perfect setting for a leisurely stroll along the shoreline or a quiet moment of contemplation. The absence of large resorts and commercial developments contributes to the beach's natural charm, allowing visitors to connect with the unspoiled beauty of Guadeloupe.

Snorkelers will find the underwater world of Plage de la Perle captivating, with vibrant coral reefs and marine life awaiting exploration. The clear visibility of the Caribbean waters enhances the snorkeling experience, making it a popular activity for those eager to discover the treasures beneath the surface.

While Plage de la Perle lacks the bustling amenities of some more commercialized beaches, this is part of its charm. Visitors often bring picnic baskets and beach essentials, creating their own little oasis on the sand. The simplicity and tranquility of Plage de la

Perle make it an ideal destination for those seeking an authentic and unspoiled beach experience.

As the sun begins to dip below the horizon, casting a warm glow over the beach, Plage de la Perle reveals its true essence—a natural pearl awaiting discovery along the shores of Guadeloupe. It's a destination that invites travelers to embrace the simplicity of a day at the beach and relish the unspoiled beauty that defines this Caribbean jewel.

Memorial ACTe

In the heart of Pointe-à-Pitre, the Memorial ACTe stands as a powerful testament to Guadeloupe's history and its profound impact on the global narrative of slavery. This cultural and educational center, opened in 2015, is dedicated to preserving and honoring the memory of those who endured the transatlantic slave trade and the legacy that continues to shape the Caribbean and beyond.

Architecturally striking, the Memorial ACTe's design mirrors the complex layers of history it aims to explore. The building's dynamic structure reflects the resilience and strength of those who faced oppression, while its interactive exhibits invite visitors to engage with the profound stories of the past. Located on the site of the former Darboussier sugar factory, the memorial's physical presence is a poignant reminder of Guadeloupe's plantation history.

The exhibits within the Memorial ACTe are both comprehensive and deeply moving. Through multimedia presentations, artifacts, and personal narratives, visitors gain insight into the harsh realities of slavery, the cultural resilience of the enslaved, and the subsequent struggles for freedom and identity. The memorial's educational programs and events foster a deeper understanding of the historical context that continues to shape the social fabric of the Caribbean.

The Memorial ACTe is not merely a static museum but a living space for reflection and dialogue. Its commitment to acknowledging the trauma of the past while promoting awareness and reconciliation is evident in its diverse programming, including lectures, performances, and community engagement initiatives. The memorial serves as a bridge between history and the present, urging visitors to confront uncomfortable truths and fostering a collective commitment to justice and equality.

For those exploring Guadeloupe, a visit to the Memorial ACTe is a profound and essential experience. It's an opportunity to engage with the complexities of the region's history, honor the resilience of its people, and contribute to ongoing conversations about social justice. The Memorial ACTe stands not only as a memorial to the past but as a beacon guiding us toward a more informed and compassionate future.

Carbet Falls

Nestled within the lush confines of Guadeloupe National Park on Basse-Terre, Carbet Falls emerges as a breathtaking natural spectacle, captivating visitors with its cascading beauty and surrounded by the tropical richness of the Caribbean rainforest. This iconic waterfall, comprising three distinct tiers, is a testament to the island's enchanting landscapes and serves as a must-visit destination for nature enthusiasts and adventure seekers alike.

Embarking on the journey to Carbet Falls is a sensory experience in itself, as the hiking trail winds through dense vegetation, echoing with the sounds of tropical birds and the rustling leaves of towering trees. The trail, well-maintained and accessible, leads explorers to various viewpoints, each unveiling a unique perspective of the falls and the verdant surroundings.

The first tier of Carbet Falls, known as "Chute du Carbet," is the most easily accessible, offering a striking introduction to the waterfall complex. Its cascading waters plunge into a pristine pool, creating an inviting setting for those seeking a refreshing dip in the midst of nature's embrace.

Venturing further along the trail, visitors encounter the second tier, aptly named "La Grande Cascade." This majestic segment features a more significant drop and a mesmerizing curtain of water that delights the senses. The lush vegetation enveloping the falls enhances the immersive experience, creating a harmonious fusion of sight and sound.

For the more adventurous souls, the third tier, "Chute du Galion," awaits at a higher elevation. This portion of Carbet Falls requires a more strenuous hike, but the reward is a panoramic view of the Caribbean Sea and the surrounding landscapes. The effort to reach this vantage point is repaid with a sense of accomplishment and a breathtaking panorama of Guadeloupe's natural beauty.

As visitors stand in awe of Carbet Falls, they are not only witnessing a captivating natural wonder but also connecting with the ecological richness of Guadeloupe. The falls stand as a testament to the importance of preserving the island's biodiversity and showcasing its allure to those eager to explore the wonders of the Caribbean rainforest.

Les Saintes

Embraced by the gentle waves of the Caribbean Sea, Les Saintes emerges as an archipelago within the embrace of Guadeloupe, offering a serene escape into a world of pristine beaches, charming villages, and panoramic views. Comprising several islands, with Terre-de-Haut and Terre-de-Bas being the most prominent, Les Saintes captivates visitors with its unspoiled beauty and tranquil ambiance.

Accessible by ferry from the mainland, the journey to Les Saintes sets the tone for a tranquil escape. As you approach the archipelago, the turquoise waters and lush hillsides welcome you to a haven where time seems to slow down. Terre-de-Haut, the main island, unveils a postcard-perfect landscape adorned with pastel-colored houses, inviting cafes, and winding streets that exude a timeless charm.

The beaches of Les Saintes, such as Anse Crawen and Pompierre, boast powdery white sands and crystalline waters, providing idyllic spots for sunbathing, swimming, and snorkeling. The unhurried pace of life on the islands encourages visitors to savor the simple joys of the Caribbean, from leisurely walks along the shore to sipping on a cool drink in a beachside café.

Exploring the picturesque village of Terre-de-Haut reveals a delightful blend of French and Creole influences in its architecture and culinary offerings. Quaint boutiques, local markets, and seafood restaurants invite visitors to experience the authentic flavors and traditions of Les Saintes. Fort Napoléon, perched atop a hill, offers panoramic views of the archipelago and provides insight into the islands' historical significance.

For those seeking a closer connection with nature, hiking trails lead to elevated viewpoints, offering breathtaking vistas of the Caribbean Sea and neighboring islands. The hike to Le Chameau, a vantage point on Terre-de-Haut, is particularly rewarding, providing a panoramic canvas of the archipelago's beauty.

Les Saintes encapsulates the essence of a tranquil Caribbean retreat, where the unhurried rhythm of island life harmonizes with the natural splendor that defines Guadeloupe. Whether you're unwinding on a secluded beach, exploring charming villages, or hiking to panoramic viewpoints, Les Saintes invites you to embrace the serene beauty and authentic charm of this hidden Caribbean gem.

Guadeloupe National Park

Nestled in the verdant embrace of Basse-Terre, Guadeloupe National Park stands as a lush sanctuary, preserving the rich biodiversity of the Caribbean. Covering over 300 square kilometers, the park is a haven for nature lovers and adventure seekers alike. Its address, Basse-Terre, makes it easily accessible for those exploring Guadeloupe, and its diverse ecosystems, from dense rainforests to volcanic peaks, create a captivating backdrop for exploration.

Getting to Guadeloupe National Park is a seamless journey, with well-marked entrances and roads leading to the heart of this natural wonder. The Route de la Traversée, a scenic road slicing through the park, provides access to some of its most iconic sites. As you venture deeper into the park, the dense foliage gives way to hiking trails, revealing the rich tapestry of flora and fauna that defines this Caribbean gem.

One of the park's prominent features is La Soufrière Volcano, the highest peak in the Lesser Antilles. The hike to the summit offers a challenging yet rewarding experience, granting panoramic views of the surrounding islands and the lush landscapes below. The park's diverse trails cater to various hiking levels, with each path leading to hidden waterfalls, sulfur springs, and captivating viewpoints.

For those fascinated by the natural world, the park is a living laboratory, home to a myriad of plant and animal species, including the raccoon-like agouti and the colorful Saint Lucian parrot. The lush vegetation creates a captivating soundtrack as you explore, with the calls of tropical birds echoing through the canopies.

A visit to Guadeloupe National Park is an immersive experience, with opportunities for birdwatching, guided hikes, and cultural encounters at the park's interpretive centers. The Maison de la Forêt provides insights into the park's ecosystems, while the Maison de la Banane delves into the cultural significance of bananas in Guadeloupe.

As you traverse the park's trails and ascend to its peaks, the immersive beauty of Guadeloupe National Park unfolds, inviting you to connect with the Caribbean's natural wonders.

La Grande Vigie

Standing proudly on the northern tip of Grande-Terre, La Grande Vigie is a dramatic coastal vantage point that offers panoramic views of the Atlantic Ocean. This elevated site, perched atop rugged cliffs, provides a breathtaking contrast to the calm turquoise waters found on other parts of the island. La Grande Vigie is not just a scenic overlook; it's a testament to the diverse landscapes that define Guadeloupe.

To reach La Grande Vigie, one can follow the winding coastal road that leads to the northernmost point of Grande-Terre. As you approach the site, the rugged beauty of the cliffs becomes apparent, showcasing the raw power of the Atlantic waves crashing against the shoreline. The journey to La Grande Vigie is as captivating as the destination itself, with the road bordered by lush vegetation and occasional glimpses of hidden coves.

Upon reaching the viewpoint, visitors are greeted by an expansive panorama of the Atlantic, where the endless horizon meets the azure sky. The sheer cliffs create a sense of grandeur, and the constant breeze from the ocean provides a refreshing respite. The natural beauty of the surroundings invites contemplation, making La Grande Vigie a serene spot for those seeking a moment of solitude or a romantic escape.

Photographers and nature enthusiasts will find La Grande Vigie to be a captivating subject, especially during the golden hours when the sunlight bathes the cliffs in a warm glow. The stark contrast between the jagged coastline and the vastness of the ocean creates a visual spectacle that is both dramatic and serene.

For those who appreciate a leisurely exploration, the area surrounding La Grande Vigie offers walking paths along the cliffs, allowing visitors to savor the coastal scenery from different angles. The rugged beauty of this northernmost point exemplifies the diverse topography that defines Guadeloupe, offering a unique perspective that complements the tropical landscapes found throughout the archipelago.

In the embrace of La Grande Vigie, one can truly appreciate the untamed beauty of Guadeloupe's coastline, where the Atlantic's powerful embrace meets the resilient cliffs of Grande-Terre. It's a destination that encourages reflection, admiration, and a deep connection with the dynamic forces of nature that shape this Caribbean jewel.

Anse du Souffleur

Tucked away on the western coast of Grande-Terre, Anse du Souffleur beckons with its pristine beauty, offering a tranquil escape along the shores of Guadeloupe. This idyllic beach, named for the gentle trade winds that grace its shores, captures the essence of the Caribbean's serene allure. With its golden sands, swaying palms, and inviting waters, Anse du Souffleur invites visitors to unwind in a secluded paradise.

Accessing Anse du Souffleur is a journey through lush landscapes, as the coastal road meanders through fields of sugar cane and tropical vegetation. Upon arrival, the beach unfolds like a hidden gem, framed by low cliffs and shaded by palm trees. The absence of large resorts and commercial developments preserves the natural charm of this coastal haven.

The golden sands of Anse du Souffleur invite sunseekers to lay down their towels and soak up the warmth of the Caribbean sun. The beach's shallow waters and gentle waves make it an ideal spot for swimming and wading, creating a tranquil environment for visitors of all ages. Those seeking a moment of solitude can find quiet corners along the shoreline, where the sounds of the ocean provide a soothing soundtrack.

The trade winds that inspired the beach's name make Anse du Souffleur a favorite among windsurfers and kiteboarders. The consistent breezes and clear waters create an ideal setting for water sports, adding an adventurous element to the serene atmosphere. The beach's natural beauty is complemented by the presence of coconut palms, providing natural shade and contributing to the tropical ambiance.

Adjacent to the beach, local eateries and beachside cafes offer a taste of Guadeloupean cuisine, allowing visitors to savor fresh seafood and tropical delights. Anse du Souffleur is not just a destination for sun and sea; it's an immersive experience that invites travelers to embrace the unhurried rhythm of island life and discover the unspoiled beauty that defines this hidden Caribbean cove.

CHAPTER 3: ACCOMMODATION OPTIONS

Embarking on your Guadeloupean adventure involves selecting accommodations that align with your travel preferences and enhance your overall experience. For those seeking the epitome of indulgence, Guadeloupe offers a selection of luxurious hotels and resorts that cater to the most discerning travelers. These upscale retreats boast idyllic beachfront locations, lavish amenities, and world-class service, providing a sumptuous backdrop for those who desire the pinnacle of Caribbean opulence.

On the flip side, budget-conscious travelers need not compromise on comfort when exploring Guadeloupe. The island caters to those seeking affordable accommodations without sacrificing quality. Budget-friendly options range from cozy guesthouses and boutique hotels to charming bed and breakfasts. These accommodations provide a wallet-friendly alternative while ensuring a cozy and welcoming atmosphere, allowing budget travelers to immerse themselves in Guadeloupe's charm without breaking the bank.

For a truly authentic and immersive experience, consider exploring unique stays and local favorites scattered across the archipelago. Guadeloupe boasts an array of charming cottages, eco-lodges, and locally-owned guesthouses that offer a genuine connection to the island's culture. Choosing one of these distinctive accommodations allows you to not only enjoy a comfortable stay but also engage with the warmth and hospitality of the local community, creating lasting memories that go beyond the typical tourist experience.

As you embark on the journey of selecting your ideal accommodation, practical tips come in handy to ensure a seamless booking process. Be sure to consider factors such as location, proximity to key attractions, and the type of experience you seek.

Additionally, leveraging online platforms, reading guest reviews, and booking in advance can enhance your chances of securing the perfect stay. With a thoughtful approach to accommodation selection, your journey through Guadeloupe is poised to be a harmonious blend of luxury, affordability, and cultural immersion.

Best Luxury Hotels and Resorts|

Embarking on a luxurious sojourn in Guadeloupe unveils a world of opulence, where the Caribbean's natural beauty converges with the finest in hospitality. The island is adorned with exquisite luxury hotels and resorts that promise an indulgent retreat for discerning travelers seeking the pinnacle of comfort and service.

La Toubana Hôtel & Spa:
Nestled on the hillside overlooking the turquoise waters of Sainte-Anne, La Toubana Hôtel & Spa stands as a premier luxury haven. Located at Pointe de la Verdure, this upscale retreat offers panoramic views of the sea and nearby islands. Guests can easily access La Toubana from the Pole Caraïbes International Airport, located approximately 25 kilometers away. Beyond the lavish accommodations, the resort boasts a spa, infinity pools, and gourmet dining options, ensuring a holistic experience for those seeking relaxation and refined pleasures.

Le Jardin Malanga:
For a tranquil retreat immersed in botanical beauty, Le Jardin Malanga in Trois-Rivières stands as a testament to luxury in a serene setting. This boutique hotel, set amidst a lush tropical garden, offers an exclusive escape on Basse-Terre. The journey to Le Jardin Malanga is a picturesque drive through the island's landscapes. Guests can indulge in personalized services, savor gourmet cuisine at the hotel's restaurant, and explore nearby attractions such as the Botanical Garden of Deshaies and the Cousteau Reserve.

La Créole Beach Hotel & Spa:
Situated on the beachfront of Gosier, La Créole Beach Hotel & Spa is an elegant retreat offering a seamless blend of Caribbean

charm and modern sophistication. The hotel is conveniently located just 7 kilometers from the Pointe-à-Pitre International Airport. With spacious rooms overlooking the sea, a rejuvenating spa, and multiple dining options, La Créole Beach Hotel provides a luxurious base for exploring nearby attractions like the Gosier Islet and the Plage de la Datcha.

Canella Beach Hotel:
Canella Beach Hotel, nestled along the coastline of Le Gosier, is a beachfront oasis that epitomizes Caribbean luxury. This upscale hotel is approximately 10 kilometers from the Pointe-à-Pitre International Airport. Guests can enjoy direct access to the beach, spacious suites with sea views, and a range of recreational activities. Canella Beach Hotel serves as a stylish retreat for those seeking relaxation and proximity to attractions such as the Musee Schoelcher and the Memorial ACTe.

Langley Resort Fort Royal:
Perched on the cliffs of Basse-Terre overlooking the Caribbean Sea, Langley Resort Fort Royal exudes charm and elegance. Located in Deshaies, this luxury resort offers a picturesque escape surrounded by tropical landscapes. The journey from the Pointe-à-Pitre International Airport unfolds through scenic routes, setting the stage for an enchanting stay. Guests can revel in spacious accommodations, enjoy beachfront dining, and explore nearby gems like the Jardin Botanique de Deshaies and the Grande Anse Beach.

Indulging in the luxury of Guadeloupe's finest accommodations ensures a harmonious blend of exquisite comfort and the enchanting allure of the Caribbean landscape.

Budget-Friendly Accommodations

Guadeloupe, with its diverse offerings, caters to budget-conscious travelers seeking affordable accommodations without compromising comfort and authenticity. Whether nestled in charming guesthouses, cozy bed and breakfasts, or boutique hotels, these budget-friendly options provide a delightful retreat for those mindful of their travel expenses.

Gîtes de France:
For an authentic and cost-effective stay, consider Gîtes de France, a network of local guesthouses and cottages scattered across the islands of Guadeloupe. These accommodations provide an intimate connection with the local culture and often feature home-cooked meals prepared with the warmth of Creole hospitality. From the vibrant markets of Pointe-à-Pitre to the serene landscapes of Sainte-Anne, Gîtes de France offers budget travelers a genuine and immersive experience.

Auberge de la Vieille Tour:
Nestled in Le Gosier, the Auberge de la Vieille Tour stands as an affordable yet charming option for those seeking a beachside retreat. Located approximately 8 kilometers from the Pointe-à-Pitre International Airport, this boutique hotel offers budget-friendly rooms with a touch of Caribbean elegance. Guests can enjoy proximity to the Gosier Islet, Plage de la Datcha, and the Casino du Gosier, ensuring a balance of relaxation and exploration without breaking the bank.

Les Bananes Vertes:
Situated in the heart of Basse-Terre in Saint-Claude, Les Bananes Vertes is a budget-friendly accommodation that combines simplicity with authenticity. This eco-lodge, surrounded by lush

greenery, provides a serene escape without compromising on environmental consciousness. Travelers seeking proximity to the La Soufrière Volcano and the hiking trails of Basse-Terre will find Les Bananes Vertes to be a welcoming haven that caters to both the budget and eco-conscious.

Hotel Amaudo:
In Saint-François, on the eastern tip of Grande-Terre, Hotel Amaudo offers an affordable retreat with a touch of sophistication. Approximately 35 kilometers from the Pointe-à-Pitre International Airport, this hotel provides budget-friendly rooms in a tranquil garden setting. Guests can explore nearby attractions such as the Pointe des Châteaux and Anse à la Gourde, immersing themselves in the natural beauty of Guadeloupe.

Résidence Hoteliere Caraibes Bonheur:
For a budget-friendly stay in Sainte-Anne, Résidence Hoteliere Caraibes Bonheur offers comfortable apartments just a short distance from the renowned Plage de la Caravelle. With easy access to the Pointe-à-Pitre International Airport, this residence provides an economical option for those seeking a self-catering stay while enjoying the sun and sea of Guadeloupe.

These budget-friendly accommodations allow travelers to experience the authentic charm of Guadeloupe without compromising on quality, providing a perfect balance for those mindful of their travel budget.

Unique Stays and Local Favorites

Guadeloupe beckons intrepid travelers to explore beyond conventional accommodations, offering a tapestry of unique stays and local favorites that promise an authentic immersion into the island's culture and charm. From cozy cottages tucked away in tropical landscapes to locally-owned guesthouses exuding warmth, these distinctive options invite visitors to create memories that go beyond the ordinary.

Ti'Coco Villa:
Nestled in the heart of Sainte-Anne, Ti'Coco Villa is a charming and unique stay that captures the essence of Creole hospitality. This locally-owned guesthouse offers intimate accommodations surrounded by lush gardens, providing a tranquil retreat just a short distance from the vibrant markets of Pointe-à-Pitre. Guests can savor homemade Creole meals, creating an authentic connection with the local way of life.

Zandoli Koko:
Embraced by the vibrant colors of Deshaies, Zandoli Koko stands as a unique bed and breakfast that seamlessly blends Caribbean authenticity with modern comfort. This artistic haven, located near the Jardin Botanique de Deshaies, reflects the passion for local art and culture. Guests can indulge in the artistic ambiance, enjoy personalized attention, and immerse themselves in the laid-back rhythms of Guadeloupe.

Karaib Pension:
For those seeking a retreat on Basse-Terre, Karaib Pension in Saint-Claude offers a unique and intimate experience. This locally-owned pension provides cozy accommodations with a personal touch, making guests feel like part of the family.

Surrounded by the lush landscapes of Basse-Terre, Karaib Pension is an ideal base for exploring the La Soufrière Volcano and the hiking trails that weave through the national park.

Les Sources du Roy:
In the heart of Saint-François, Les Sources du Roy presents a unique concept that combines eco-lodging with a touch of luxury. This eco-responsible property embraces sustainable practices while providing guests with a serene and comfortable stay. The proximity to the Pointe des Châteaux and the turquoise waters of the Atlantic adds to the allure of this locally-favored accommodation.

Chez Mirella:
Nestled in the picturesque village of Terre-de-Bas in Les Saintes, Chez Mirella embodies the charm of a local favorite. This welcoming guesthouse offers simple yet comfortable accommodations, allowing guests to experience the unhurried pace of island life. With personalized service and a location that allows easy exploration of the Les Saintes archipelago, Chez Mirella captures the essence of local hospitality.

Choosing one of these unique stays and local favorites in Guadeloupe offers travelers the opportunity to go beyond the ordinary, creating memories that resonate with the island's culture, warmth, and distinctive charm.

Practical Tips for Booking Accommodations

Navigating the process of booking accommodations in Guadeloupe requires a thoughtful approach to ensure a seamless and enjoyable stay. Here are some practical tips to consider when securing your lodging in this Caribbean paradise:

Consider Location Wisely:
Guadeloupe comprises several islands, each with its unique character. Before booking, consider the location that aligns with your interests. Basse-Terre offers lush landscapes and hiking opportunities, Grande-Terre boasts beautiful beaches, and Les Saintes provides a tranquil island escape. Ensure your accommodation is conveniently located for the activities you have in mind.

Read Guest Reviews:
Leverage the wealth of information available through online platforms. Reading guest reviews can provide valuable insights into the quality of accommodations, service, and overall experience. Look for reviews that align with your priorities, whether it be cleanliness, hospitality, or proximity to attractions.

Book in Advance, Especially in Peak Seasons:
Guadeloupe experiences peak tourist seasons, particularly during the winter months. To secure your preferred accommodation and potentially benefit from lower rates, consider booking well in advance. This is especially crucial if you plan to visit during popular times like the Christmas holidays or Carnival season.

Explore Different Accommodation Types:

Guadeloupe offers a diverse range of accommodations, from luxurious resorts to charming guesthouses and unique eco-lodges. Explore different types of lodging to find one that aligns with your preferences and budget. Consider options like Gîtes de France for an authentic local experience or boutique hotels for a touch of Caribbean elegance.

Check for Special Deals and Packages:
Before confirming your reservation, check for any special deals, discounts, or packages offered by the accommodation. Some establishments provide promotions for longer stays, early bookings, or specific travel periods. This can be an opportunity to optimize your budget and enhance your overall experience.

Understand Cancellation Policies:
Be sure to carefully review the accommodation's cancellation policies before finalizing your booking. Understand the terms and conditions regarding cancellations, modifications, and potential fees. This knowledge can prove invaluable in case unexpected changes to your travel plans arise.

Verify Amenities and Services:
Ensure that the accommodation meets your expectations by verifying the provided amenities and services. If certain features are crucial to your stay, such as Wi-Fi, air conditioning, or specific facilities, confirm their availability beforehand. This proactive approach ensures a comfortable and satisfying experience.

Connect with Locals for Recommendations:
Engage with the local community or fellow travelers for firsthand recommendations on accommodations. Local insights can uncover hidden gems, unique stays, or budget-friendly options

that might not be as prominent on popular booking platforms. Platforms like social media travel groups or forums can be valuable resources.

By incorporating these practical tips into your accommodation booking process, you can optimize your stay in Guadeloupe, aligning your lodgings with your preferences and ensuring a memorable Caribbean experience.

CHAPTER 4: DINING AND CUISINE

Embarking on a culinary journey in Guadeloupe is a delightful exploration of flavors, where each meal becomes a vibrant expression of the island's rich cultural tapestry. Begin your culinary adventure at the Marché de Sainte-Anne, a bustling market that beckons with an array of fresh produce, spices, and local specialties. This vibrant marketplace is not just a venue for acquiring ingredients; it's a cultural immersion where the vibrant colors and fragrances set the stage for the gastronomic delights that await.

As the sun dips below the horizon, venture to Le Ti'Punch Bar, where island elixirs take center stage. Sipping on a Ti'Punch, a quintessential Guadeloupean cocktail, becomes an essential part of the evening ritual. This laid-back bar offers a relaxed ambiance, inviting both locals and visitors to unwind with a sip of rum infused with sugarcane and a twist of lime. The bar serves not just drinks but an experience, fostering connections and conversations against the backdrop of the Caribbean breeze.

Guadeloupe's culinary scene extends beyond casual markets and bars to an array of restaurants and eateries that showcase the diversity of the island's gastronomy. From quaint Creole bistros to upscale seafood establishments, the best restaurants in Guadeloupe offer a symphony of flavors. Each dish becomes a masterpiece, blending French culinary finesse with Caribbean ingredients, resulting in a culinary tapestry that mirrors the island's cultural fusion.

Indulge in the local flavors and must-try dishes that define Guadeloupe's gastronomic identity. From accras, savory fritters often featuring saltfish, to boudin, a spicy blood sausage that exemplifies the Creole palate, the island's cuisine captivates the taste buds with its bold and aromatic profiles. Dive into seafood delights like court-bouillon, a fish stew brimming with herbs and spices, or colombo, a curry-infused dish that reflects the Indian influences embedded in Guadeloupe's culinary heritage.

Amidst the gastronomic journey, it's essential to embrace the dining etiquette that permeates Guadeloupean culture. Meals are not just sustenance; they are communal experiences marked by conviviality and appreciation. Engage in the unhurried rhythm of dining, savoring each bite with an appreciation for the fusion of flavors and the cultural significance embedded in every dish.

The island's culinary landscape transcends mere sustenance; it's a celebration of history, diversity, and the joy of sharing a meal with those who embrace the warmth of Guadeloupean hospitality.

Marché de Sainte-Anne: A Culinary Adventure

Embarking on a culinary adventure in Guadeloupe finds its epicenter at the Marché de Sainte-Anne, a vibrant marketplace that encapsulates the essence of the island's gastronomic delights. This bustling market, located in the heart of Sainte-Anne, is more than a venue for purchasing fresh produce and local specialties; it's a sensory journey into the heart of Guadeloupean culture.

Navigating the vibrant stalls of Marché de Sainte-Anne immerses visitors in a kaleidoscope of colors, aromas, and flavors. The air is filled with the fragrance of exotic spices, tropical fruits, and the ocean's bounty. Vendors proudly display an array of fresh produce, from vibrant Creole peppers to succulent pineapples and locally caught fish glistening on ice. It's a feast for the senses, where the visual spectacle of the market is just a prelude to the culinary treasures that await.

Local artisans and farmers converge at the market, offering a diverse array of products that reflect Guadeloupe's agricultural richness. Visitors can engage in friendly banter with vendors, gaining insights into traditional cooking methods, regional specialties, and the significance of each ingredient in Creole cuisine. The Marché de Sainte-Anne transcends the transactional; it becomes a cultural exchange where locals and travelers share a mutual appreciation for the island's culinary heritage.

As you weave through the lively atmosphere, don't miss the opportunity to sample the market's street food delights. From accras, delectable fritters bursting with flavor, to coconut-based treats and freshly squeezed sugarcane juice, every corner of the market beckons with a new culinary discovery. Marché de Sainte-Anne isn't just a place to shop; it's an immersive culinary adventure, inviting you to taste, learn, and savor the authentic flavors that define Guadeloupe's gastronomic identity.

Le Ti'Punch Bar: Sipping Island Elixirs

Amidst the enchanting ambiance of Guadeloupe, a visit to Le Ti'Punch Bar becomes a captivating journey into the art of sipping island elixirs. Nestled in the heart of this Caribbean paradise, the bar is more than just a place to enjoy a drink; it's a celebration of the island's iconic beverage, the Ti'Punch. This laid-back establishment invites patrons to unwind, sip, and revel in the convivial spirit of Guadeloupean life.

As the sun sets over the horizon, Le Ti'Punch Bar comes alive with the rhythmic sounds of local music and the clinking of glasses. The Ti'Punch, a beloved Guadeloupean cocktail, takes center stage, offering a simple yet profound experience. The concoction of aged rum, sugarcane syrup, and a splash of lime captures the essence of the Caribbean, embodying the relaxed and unhurried pace of island living.

The bar itself is a haven of authenticity, adorned with tropical decor and exuding the charm of Creole hospitality. Locals and visitors alike gather here to share stories, connect with fellow travelers, and immerse themselves in the laid-back atmosphere. The Ti'Punch becomes more than a drink; it becomes a cultural bridge, uniting people from different corners of the world in a toast to the beauty of Guadeloupe.

Le Ti'Punch Bar isn't merely a stop for a refreshing beverage; it's an invitation to savor the island's elixirs in the company of kindred spirits. Whether perched at the bar, on a seaside terrace, or under the swaying palms, each sip becomes a moment of communion with the spirit of Guadeloupe. So, let the cool breeze carry the scent of rum and lime, and allow the Ti'Punch to be not just a drink but a sensory voyage into the heart of this enchanting Caribbean destination.

Best Restaurants and Eateries

Embarking on a culinary journey in Guadeloupe is a feast for the senses, and the island's vibrant gastronomic scene is punctuated by a myriad of restaurants and eateries that promise an extraordinary dining experience. From beachside bistros to hidden gems tucked away in lush landscapes, Guadeloupe's culinary tapestry is as diverse as the landscapes that surround it. Here's a curated list of some of the best restaurants and eateries that beckon with the promise of exquisite flavors and memorable moments.

Le Touloulou:
Nestled in the charming village of Sainte-Anne, Le Touloulou is a beachfront gem that captures the essence of Creole cuisine. With its toes in the sand and a view of the turquoise sea, this restaurant offers a delectable blend of fresh seafood, tropical fruits, and aromatic spices. The laid-back atmosphere and culinary artistry make Le Touloulou a must-visit for those seeking an authentic taste of Guadeloupe.

La Canne à Sucre:
Located in Gosier, La Canne à Sucre is a culinary haven that marries French elegance with Caribbean flair. Set within a charming colonial-style house, the restaurant provides a refined dining experience. From exquisite seafood dishes to inventive Creole-inspired creations, La Canne à Sucre is a gastronomic delight that invites patrons to savor the fusion of flavors in an intimate setting.

Chez Christine:
Tucked away in the heart of Deshaies, Chez Christine is a local favorite known for its unpretentious charm and mouthwatering

Creole dishes. This family-run restaurant embodies the spirit of Guadeloupean hospitality, serving up homely and comforting meals that reflect the island's culinary traditions. The welcoming ambiance and authenticity make Chez Christine a beloved spot for both locals and visitors.

Le Mahina:
Situated in Saint-François, Le Mahina stands out as an elegant dining destination overlooking the marina. This upscale restaurant specializes in seafood delicacies, prepared with precision and flair. The refined atmosphere, attentive service, and a menu showcasing the bounty of the sea make Le Mahina a top choice for those seeking a sophisticated culinary experience.

Amerindiens Café:
Immerse yourself in the unique ambiance of Amerindiens Café, nestled in the heart of Le Moule. This charming eatery combines a vintage setting with a menu inspired by indigenous Caribbean flavors. From traditional casseroles to grilled specialties, Amerindiens Café offers a culinary journey that pays homage to Guadeloupe's cultural heritage.

Exploring these best restaurants and eateries in Guadeloupe is not just a gastronomic adventure; it's an invitation to savor the diverse flavors that define the island's culinary landscape. Each establishment on this list contributes to the rich tapestry of tastes that make dining in Guadeloupe an unforgettable experience.

Local Flavors and Must-Try Dishes

Delving into the culinary scene of Guadeloupe unveils a treasure trove of local flavors and must-try dishes that embody the rich tapestry of Caribbean cuisine. From savory street food to hearty Creole classics, here's a curated guide to the authentic flavors that define the gastronomic identity of Guadeloupe.

Accras:
Kickstart your culinary exploration with accras, delectable fritters that are a staple of Guadeloupean street food. These savory bites feature a tantalizing blend of saltfish, herbs, and spices, deep-fried to golden perfection. Often enjoyed as a snack or appetizer, accras encapsulate the bold and aromatic profile of Creole cuisine.

Colombo:
A dish with roots in Indian cuisine, colombo is a flavorful curry-infused creation that has become a hallmark of Guadeloupean dining. Typically prepared with chicken, goat, or fish, colombo features a medley of spices such as cumin, coriander, and turmeric. Served with rice or root vegetables, this aromatic dish offers a taste of the diverse cultural influences that shape Guadeloupean cooking.

Boudin:
Spice enthusiasts will appreciate boudin, a spicy blood sausage that adds a kick to Guadeloupe's culinary repertoire. This Creole delicacy is crafted with a blend of pig's blood, rice, and aromatic spices, resulting in a robust and flavorful sausage. Often enjoyed grilled or as part of a traditional Creole dish, boudin showcases the island's penchant for bold and hearty flavors.

Court-Bouillon:
Seafood lovers rejoice in the flavors of court-bouillon, a fish stew that exemplifies Guadeloupean coastal cuisine. Prepared with a medley of herbs, tomatoes, and spices, this aromatic dish showcases the freshest catches from the Caribbean waters. Served with rice or bread, court-bouillon is a culinary journey into the heart of Guadeloupe's maritime traditions.

Dombrés aux Fruits de Mer:
Guadeloupe's culinary creativity shines in dombrés aux fruits de mer, a dish that combines dumplings with an array of fresh seafood. These fluffy dumplings, often infused with coconut milk, are simmered in a savory seafood broth, creating a harmonious blend of textures and flavors. It's a comforting and indulgent dish that pays homage to the island's bountiful marine resources.

Exploring the local flavors and must-try dishes of Guadeloupe is not just a culinary adventure; it's a cultural immersion into the vibrant and diverse influences that have shaped the island's gastronomy. Each bite is a testament to the warmth, history, and passion that define Guadeloupean cooking.

Dining Etiquette

Engaging in dining experiences in Guadeloupe involves not only savoring the flavors but also embracing the cultural nuances that accompany the island's dining etiquette. As you embark on your culinary journey, consider these essential dining etiquettes to fully immerse yourself in the warmth of Guadeloupean hospitality:

Laid-Back Pacing:
Guadeloupeans appreciate a relaxed and unhurried approach to dining. Meals are not just about nourishment; they are a communal experience meant to be enjoyed at a leisurely pace. Embrace the laid-back rhythm, savoring each bite and engaging in unhurried conversations with your fellow diners.

Communal Dining:
Many dining experiences in Guadeloupe are communal, especially in family settings or local eateries. It's common for dishes to be served family-style, encouraging sharing and a sense of togetherness. Embrace this communal aspect, pass dishes around, and enjoy the convivial atmosphere.

Greetings and Politeness:
Begin your meal with a courteous "Bonjour" or "Bonsoir," depending on the time of day. Politeness and warm greetings are integral to Guadeloupean culture. Take a moment to exchange pleasantries with your dining companions and the restaurant staff to set a positive tone for the meal.

Respecting Meal Times:
Guadeloupeans adhere to set meal times, with lunch typically being the main meal of the day. It's advisable to plan your meals

accordingly and be mindful of local schedules. Restaurants may close during certain hours, especially in the afternoon, so checking opening times is a thoughtful gesture.

Tipping Practices:
Tipping is appreciated in Guadeloupe, and it is customary to leave a small gratuity for good service. While a service charge may be included in some bills, adding a bit extra for exceptional service is a common practice. Gratitude is expressed with a simple "merci" as you settle your bill.

Dress Code:
The dress code in Guadeloupe is generally casual, especially in beachside restaurants and local eateries. However, some upscale establishments may have a more formal dress code, so it's advisable to check in advance. Embrace the island's relaxed style while being mindful of specific venue requirements.

Exploring Local Specialties:
Part of the dining etiquette in Guadeloupe involves an openness to trying local specialties. Embrace the opportunity to explore the diverse flavors the island has to offer. Don't hesitate to ask for recommendations or guidance on navigating the menu, and be open to the culinary surprises that await.

By incorporating these dining etiquettes into your culinary adventures, you not only enhance your gastronomic experience but also connect with the heart of Guadeloupean culture, where meals are a celebration of community, warmth, and shared joy.

CHAPTER 5: THINGS TO DO AND OUTDOOR ACTIVITIES

Embarking on a journey through the outdoor wonders of Guadeloupe unfolds a tapestry of experiences that span from the heights of volcanic trails to the depths of crystal-clear waters. Hiking enthusiasts find their thrill in conquering the trails of La Soufrière, the iconic volcano that graces Basse-Terre. The varied trails offer not just breathtaking panoramas but also a connection with the island's geological wonders. From the lush rainforests to the lunar landscapes near the summit, the trails of La Soufrière promise both challenges and rewards for adventurers seeking a rendezvous with nature.

Guadeloupe's aquatic realm beckons with an array of water adventures that go beyond the surface. Diving enthusiasts plunge into the mesmerizing world beneath, exploring vibrant coral reefs teeming with marine life. Snorkeling excursions reveal a kaleidoscope of colors as tropical fish dart through translucent waters. From the Pigeon Islands' marine reserve to the Cousteau Reserve, Guadeloupe's underwater treasures captivate those seeking an aquatic escapade.

Venturing to the horizon leads to the enchanting Les Saintes Islands, an archipelago that extends an invitation beyond the ordinary. Discovering Les Saintes is not just a journey across the sea but a voyage into a realm where time seems to slow. Tranquil beaches, charming villages, and panoramic viewpoints await exploration. The rich history and captivating landscapes of Terre-de-Haut and Terre-de-Bas offer a glimpse into the cultural tapestry of this island paradise.

For those seeking the simple joys of sun and sand, Guadeloupe's pristine beaches unfold as idyllic playgrounds. From the golden shores of Grande-Anse to the serene coves of Sainte-Anne, the beaches invite both relaxation and recreation. Sunbathers bask in the warmth, while water enthusiasts engage in an array of activities, from paddleboarding along the coast to building sandcastles with the family. The beaches of Guadeloupe embody the essence of leisure, providing a picturesque backdrop for moments of tranquility and joy.

In the outdoor realm of Guadeloupe, each activity is a brushstroke on the canvas of an island waiting to be explored. From the heights of volcanic peaks to the depths of azure waters, the outdoor wonders of Guadeloupe promise a diverse and immersive experience for adventurers and leisure seekers alike.

Hiking La Soufrière: Trails and Thrills

Embarking on the exhilarating adventure of hiking La Soufrière, Guadeloupe's iconic volcano, promises both scenic trails and thrilling experiences. Located in Basse-Terre, the volcano is a captivating natural landmark with multiple trails catering to various skill levels.

To reach La Soufrière, make your way to the town of Saint-Claude in Basse-Terre. The trailhead is conveniently accessible from here. If you're coming from Pointe-à-Pitre, follow the N1 road south towards Basse-Terre, and then take the D11 road to Saint-Claude. Signs will guide you to the starting point of the hiking trails.

One of the popular trails is the Chemin des Dames, a moderately challenging route that unveils the lush beauty of Guadeloupe's rainforest. As you ascend, the trail offers panoramic vistas, leading you through a diverse landscape of dense vegetation and volcanic rocks. The final stretch to the summit provides a surreal experience as you emerge above the tree line, surrounded by otherworldly lunar landscapes.

At the summit, stand in awe of the panoramic views that stretch across Basse-Terre and beyond. The volcanic crater adds a touch of drama to the scene, reminding hikers of the geological forces at play. Be sure to check the weather conditions before embarking on the hike, and pack essentials such as water, snacks, and sturdy footwear.

Hiking La Soufrière is not just a physical challenge; it's an opportunity to connect with the natural wonders of Guadeloupe. The trails and thrills of this volcanic adventure offer a memorable experience, making it a must-do activity for nature enthusiasts and those seeking a taste of the Caribbean's wild beauty.

Water Adventures: Diving, Snorkeling, and More

Dive into the aquatic wonders of Guadeloupe, where water adventures beckon with a vibrant tapestry of marine life and crystal-clear depths. Whether you're a seasoned diver or a snorkeling enthusiast, the azure waters surrounding the islands promise an underwater paradise waiting to be explored.

For diving enthusiasts, the Cousteau Reserve near Pigeon Islands is a haven of biodiversity. Named after the legendary Jacques Cousteau, this marine reserve boasts coral reefs teeming with colorful fish, rays, and sea turtles. Dive centers in Malendure offer guided excursions, providing an opportunity to explore the submerged world and discover the allure of Guadeloupe's underwater realm.

If snorkeling is more your speed, the pristine beaches and coral-rich coves of Guadeloupe invite you to witness the mesmerizing marine life up close. Equip yourself with a mask and fins, and venture into the shallow waters of places like Plage de la Caravelle or the Pigeon Islands. Here, schools of tropical fish, vibrant corals, and the occasional sea turtle create a captivating underwater spectacle.

Beyond diving and snorkeling, Guadeloupe offers a myriad of water adventures for every taste. Kayak through the mangroves of Grand Cul-de-Sac Marin, discovering the ecological wonders of this coastal ecosystem. Paddleboarding along the shores of Anse à la Barque or Malendure Bay provides a serene experience, allowing you to soak in the coastal beauty at your own pace.

For the thrill-seekers, windsurfing and kiteboarding opportunities abound at spots like Sainte-Anne and Le Moule, where steady trade winds create ideal conditions for these exhilarating water sports. Lessons and equipment rentals are available for those looking to harness the power of the wind and waves.

Whether you're exploring vibrant coral gardens beneath the surface, paddling through mangrove lagoons, or riding the winds on a kiteboard, Guadeloupe's water adventures promise an immersive experience for water lovers of all levels. The aquatic wonders that surround the islands invite you to dive in, explore, and create unforgettable memories in the heart of the Caribbean Sea.

Exploring Les Saintes Islands: Beyond the Horizon

Embark on a voyage beyond the horizon to discover the enchanting Les Saintes Islands, an archipelago that unveils a world of tranquility, charm, and natural beauty. Located off the southern coast of Guadeloupe, Les Saintes comprises several islands, with Terre-de-Haut and Terre-de-Bas being the most prominent.

To reach Les Saintes, take a short ferry ride from the town of Trois-Rivières on the southern tip of Basse-Terre. The journey itself becomes a scenic prelude to the islands' beauty as you traverse the azure waters of the Caribbean Sea.

Terre-de-Haut, the main island, welcomes visitors with its postcard-perfect landscapes. Stroll through the charming village, where red-roofed houses and narrow streets exude a European flair. Fort Napoléon, perched atop a hill, offers panoramic views of the island and the surrounding sea. The museum within the fort provides insights into the archipelago's history.

For a moment of serenity, head to Anse Crawen, a secluded beach with powdery white sand and clear turquoise waters. It's a perfect spot to unwind and appreciate the unspoiled beauty of Les Saintes.

Terre-de-Bas, while quieter, is equally captivating. The island is renowned for its hiking trails, leading to scenic viewpoints such as Morne Morel, where the panoramic vistas are a testament to the untouched natural splendor of Les Saintes.

Exploring Les Saintes goes beyond the conventional tourist experience. Engage with the locals, sample fresh seafood at seaside eateries, and embrace the unhurried pace of island life. Snorkeling enthusiasts can discover vibrant marine life around Pain de Sucre, a small islet near Terre-de-Haut.

The Les Saintes Islands present a canvas of diverse experiences, from historical explorations to moments of quiet contemplation on pristine beaches. As you venture beyond the horizon to these captivating isles, you'll find that Les Saintes beckon with a promise of genuine tranquility and an authentic taste of Caribbean island life.

Beach Activities: Relaxation and Recreation

Embrace the sun-kissed shores of Guadeloupe as you indulge in a spectrum of beach activities that seamlessly blend relaxation with recreation. Each beach is a canvas of natural beauty, inviting both tranquility seekers and adventure enthusiasts to experience the coastal charms of this Caribbean paradise.

Grande-Anse:
Begin your beach escapades at Grande-Anse, a pristine stretch of golden sand framed by lush vegetation. To reach this idyllic spot on Basse-Terre, take the D26 road from Deshaies. Grande-Anse is not only a haven for sunbathers but also a hub for water activities. Dip your toes in the warm Caribbean waters or engage in paddleboarding along the shoreline for a leisurely coastal exploration.

Sainte-Anne:
Venture to Sainte-Anne, a postcard-perfect destination with turquoise waters and powdery white sand. Accessible from Pointe-à-Pitre by the N4 and D118 roads, Sainte-Anne offers a picturesque setting for beach enthusiasts. Relax under the shade of palm trees, indulge in beachside picnics, or partake in beach volleyball for a spirited day in the sun.

Plage de la Caravelle:
For those seeking a balance of tranquility and water sports, Plage de la Caravelle is an ideal choice. Nestled near Saint-François on Grande-Terre, this beach can be reached via the D118 road. Bask in the serene ambiance, or embark on windsurfing adventures with the steady trade winds that grace the coastline.

Anse du Souffleur:
To experience the charm of a secluded beach, visit Anse du Souffleur in Port-Louis on Grande-Terre. Take the D123 road from Pointe-à-Pitre for a tranquil journey to this hidden gem. Renowned for its serene waters, Anse du Souffleur is an ideal spot for swimming and snorkeling. Enjoy a leisurely day under the swaying palms, taking in the unspoiled beauty of this coastal retreat.

Plage de la Perle:
Conclude your beach-hopping adventure at Plage de la Perle, located near Deshaies on Basse-Terre. Accessible via the D26 road, this beach is characterized by its black sand and relaxed atmosphere. Unwind with a book under a beach umbrella or partake in kayaking for a refreshing coastal exploration.

Guadeloupe's beaches are not just destinations; they are invitations to savor the simplicity of sun, sand, and sea. Whether you're seeking a quiet retreat or an active day by the shore, each beach offers a unique palette of experiences, inviting you to create cherished moments along the coastline of this tropical haven.

CHAPTER 6: ART, CULTURE AND ENTERTAINMENT

Immerse yourself in the vibrant tapestry of art, culture, and entertainment that defines Guadeloupe, where each facet unveils a unique expression of the island's rich heritage. Local arts and crafts serve as living canvases, with skilled artisans creating masterpieces that reflect the soul of Guadeloupean creativity. Stroll through the colorful markets, such as the Sainte-Anne Craft Market, where handcrafted treasures tell stories of tradition and innovation. From intricately woven straw hats to vividly painted ceramics, these locally crafted works of art are more than souvenirs; they are windows into the island's cultural narrative.

Journey into the heart of Guadeloupe's cultural landscape by exploring its museums and galleries, where history and artistic expression intertwine. The Memorial ACTe in Pointe-à-Pitre stands as a poignant testament to the island's past, addressing the complexities of slavery and the resilience of the human spirit. Meanwhile, galleries like the Schoelcher Museum in Pointe-à-Pitre showcase the works of esteemed artists, offering a visual feast for those seeking to connect with Guadeloupe's contemporary art scene.

As the sun sets, Guadeloupe's vibrant nightlife and entertainment scene come to life. From beachside bars in Sainte-Anne, where the rhythmic beats of Caribbean music set the tone, to the lively atmosphere of Le Gosier's entertainment district, the island pulsates with energy. Join locals and fellow travelers in dance, laughter, and the shared joy of celebrating life. The sounds of zouk and reggae fill the air, creating an ambiance where every night out becomes a memorable chapter in your Guadeloupean adventure.

Amidst the lively beats and artistic expressions, Guadeloupe's festivals and events provide a cultural kaleidoscope that enriches the visitor's experience. From the Carnival of Guadeloupe, a vibrant extravaganza of costumes and music, to the Terre de Blues Festival in Marie-Galante, where the soulful notes of blues echo through the Caribbean night, these events showcase the island's dynamism and the spirit of its people. It's an invitation to join the festivities, to dance, to revel, and to become part of the cultural heartbeat of Guadeloupe.

Local Arts and Crafts

Guadeloupe's local arts and crafts scene is a vibrant celebration of creativity and cultural heritage. As you explore the island, you'll encounter a kaleidoscope of handcrafted treasures that reflect the skill, tradition, and artistic flair of the Guadeloupean people. From the bustling markets to quaint artisan shops, each piece tells a story, offering visitors a tangible connection to the island's soul.

Wander through the Sainte-Anne Craft Market, where artisans showcase their expertise in traditional crafts. Intricately woven straw hats and baskets catch the eye, displaying the artistry passed down through generations. Local woodcarvers skillfully carve sculptures and utensils, while vibrant ceramics adorned with Caribbean motifs beckon as unique keepsakes. These locally crafted treasures not only serve as souvenirs but also as tangible expressions of Guadeloupe's cultural richness.

Step into the world of Madras fabric, a brightly colored textile that holds deep cultural significance. Local seamstresses skillfully fashion Madras into clothing, accessories, and decorative items, infusing each piece with a burst of color and a touch of Creole charm. Whether it's a stylish dress, a headwrap, or a decorative tablecloth, Madras creations embody the spirit of Guadeloupean aesthetics and traditions.

Beyond the markets, visit artisan workshops where you can witness the creation process firsthand. Skilled craftsmen and women transform raw materials into works of art, showcasing the intricate techniques passed down through the ages. Engaging with local artisans provides not just an opportunity to purchase unique pieces but also a chance to understand the stories behind the craftsmanship, fostering a deeper appreciation for Guadeloupe's artistic legacy.

Guadeloupe's local arts and crafts scene is a living testament to the island's cultural diversity and creative spirit. Each handmade creation is a brushstroke in the canvas of Guadeloupean identity, inviting visitors to take home more than just a souvenir but a piece of the island's artistic soul.

Museums and Galleries

Immerse yourself in the captivating world of Guadeloupe's museums and galleries, where the island's rich history, artistic expressions, and cultural narratives come to life. Explore these cultural havens to gain deeper insights into Guadeloupe's past, appreciate contemporary artistry, and engage with the diverse facets of the island's identity.

Memorial ACTe, Pointe-à-Pitre:
Delve into the poignant history of Guadeloupe at the Memorial ACTe. This museum, situated in Pointe-à-Pitre, is a powerful testament to the impact of slavery on the Caribbean region. Through fully immersive exhibitions, multimedia presentations, and intriguing displays, the Memorial ACTe invites visitors to reflect on the complex legacy of this historical period.

Schoelcher Museum, Pointe-à-Pitre:
Immerse yourself in the world of Victor Schoelcher, a prominent abolitionist, at the Schoelcher Museum. Housed in a grand building in Pointe-à-Pitre, this museum showcases the life and contributions of Schoelcher, whose efforts were instrumental in the abolition of slavery in the French colonies. The museum's extensive collection includes artifacts, documents, and personal belongings that offer a glimpse into this pivotal era.

Saint John Perse Museum, Pointe-à-Pitre:
Explore the literary and cultural heritage of Guadeloupe at the Saint John Perse Museum. Dedicated to the Nobel Prize-winning poet Alexis Léger, who wrote under the pseudonym Saint John Perse, the museum houses a remarkable collection of manuscripts, letters, and personal effects. Discover the poet's

influence on Caribbean literature and his reflections on identity, exile, and the human condition.

Arté Gallery, Basse-Terre:
Immerse yourself in the contemporary art scene of Guadeloupe at Arté Gallery in Basse-Terre. This dynamic space showcases the works of local and international artists, providing a platform for creative expression. From paintings and sculptures to multimedia installations, Arté Gallery offers a diverse visual experience that reflects the evolving cultural landscape of the island.

Exploring Guadeloupe's museums and galleries is not just a journey through time and artistic expression; it's an invitation to engage with the multifaceted layers of the island's identity. Whether delving into the complexities of history or appreciating the vibrancy of contemporary art, each museum and gallery adds a unique brushstroke to the cultural canvas of Guadeloupe.

Festivals and Events

Guadeloupe comes alive with a rhythmic heartbeat of celebrations, festivals, and events that showcase the island's vibrant culture and lively spirit. From pulsating music and colorful parades to cultural showcases, these festivities offer a unique opportunity to immerse yourself in the joyous traditions of the Caribbean.

Carnival of Guadeloupe:
Join the vivacious Carnival of Guadeloupe, a spectacle of music, dance, and elaborate costumes that takes to the streets each year. The festivities, influenced by African, European, and Caribbean traditions, unfold in a whirlwind of color and rhythm. Locals and visitors alike partake in the lively parades, marked by traditional masquerade bands, spirited zouk music, and the infectious energy that defines this annual celebration.

Terre de Blues Festival, Marie-Galante:
Venture to Marie-Galante for the Terre de Blues Festival, an internationally acclaimed event that celebrates the soulful notes of blues against the backdrop of the Caribbean Sea. Held in the charming town of Grand-Bourg, this festival attracts renowned musicians from around the world, creating an atmospheric blend of music, culture, and community. Revel in the open-air concerts that carry the soulful tunes across the island.

Gwoka Festival, Sainte-Anne:
Immerse yourself in the rhythms of Gwoka, a traditional Guadeloupean music genre, at the Gwoka Festival in Sainte-Anne. This vibrant celebration pays homage to the island's musical heritage, featuring drumming competitions, dance performances, and interactive workshops. The festival serves as a

dynamic platform for both seasoned Gwoka enthusiasts and those eager to explore the roots of Guadeloupean music.

Guadeloupe International Film Festival:
Engage with the cinematic arts at the Guadeloupe International Film Festival, where filmmakers, actors, and cinephiles converge to celebrate the diverse voices of Caribbean and international cinema. Screenings, discussions, and cultural events unfold in various locations across the islands, offering a cinematic journey that reflects the global perspectives woven into the fabric of Guadeloupe.

As you navigate the calendar of festivals and events in Guadeloupe, each celebration becomes a gateway to the heart of the island's cultural identity. Whether reveling in the exuberance of Carnival, swaying to the blues in Marie-Galante, drumming to the beats of Gwoka, or immersing yourself in the world of cinema, Guadeloupe's festivals offer an unforgettable tapestry of experiences that resonate with the warmth and vibrancy of Caribbean culture.

Nightlife and Entertainment

As the sun sets over the Caribbean horizon, Guadeloupe transforms into a vibrant tapestry of nightlife and entertainment, offering a kaleidoscope of experiences that cater to diverse tastes. From beachside bars pulsating with rhythmic beats to lively districts alive with the spirit of celebration, Guadeloupe's nightlife is a rhythmic dance of joy under the starlit skies.

Le Gosier Entertainment District:
Step into the heart of Guadeloupe's nightlife at Le Gosier, a bustling entertainment district that comes alive after dark. Here, a myriad of bars, clubs, and open-air venues offer a dynamic blend of music genres, from zouk and reggae to salsa and electronic beats. Join the locals and fellow travelers in the dance, savoring the infectious energy that permeates the night.

Beachside Bars in Sainte-Anne:
For a more laid-back but equally enchanting evening, head to the beachside bars in Sainte-Anne. Sink your toes into the sand as you sip on tropical cocktails, enjoying the rhythmic sounds of local musicians. The ambiance is relaxed, the moonlight reflecting on the gentle waves, creating a tranquil setting for a memorable night by the sea.

Live Music in Pointe-à-Pitre:
Explore the streets of Pointe-à-Pitre, where you'll discover venues hosting live music performances that cater to diverse tastes. From intimate jazz clubs to larger concert spaces, Pointe-à-Pitre's music scene embraces a spectrum of genres, ensuring there's something for everyone. Immerse yourself in the melodies, surrounded by the warm camaraderie of fellow music enthusiasts.

Rum Tasting and Local Hangouts:
Indulge in the island's spirit by exploring local rum bars and tasting sessions. Guadeloupe is known for its exceptional rums, and sampling different varieties becomes a delightful part of the nightlife experience. Engage with locals in charming rum bars, sharing stories and laughter over glasses of the island's finest.

Guadeloupe's nightlife is a celebration of life, where the rhythms of the Caribbean infuse every corner with an irresistible energy. Whether you choose to dance the night away in Le Gosier, unwind at beachside bars, enjoy live music in Pointe-à-Pitre, or savor the flavors of local rums, the island's nightlife invites you to become part of a spirited and unforgettable Caribbean soirée.

Local Markets, Shopping, and Souvenirs

Embark on a delightful journey through Guadeloupe's local markets, where the vibrant colors, enticing aromas, and lively atmosphere create a sensory experience like no other. These markets are not just places to shop; they are cultural hubs where the island's flavors, crafts, and traditions come together, inviting you to explore and take home a piece of Guadeloupe.

Sainte-Anne Craft Market:
Begin your shopping adventure at the Sainte-Anne Craft Market, a bustling hub of local artisans and vendors. Here, vibrant stalls showcase a kaleidoscope of handcrafted treasures, from straw hats and baskets to intricately painted ceramics. Dive into the rhythm of Creole life as you meander through the market, engaging with skilled craftsmen and women who breathe life into their creations. Take home a piece of Guadeloupean craftsmanship, a tangible reminder of the island's artistic spirit.

Pointe-à-Pitre Spice Market:
Explore the vibrant Pointe-à-Pitre Spice Market, where the air is filled with the intoxicating scents of local spices, herbs, and exotic produce. Navigate through the lively stalls offering an array of aromatic spices, hot sauces, and tropical fruits. Engage with the vendors to learn about the diverse flavors that define Guadeloupean cuisine. Whether you're a culinary enthusiast or seeking a unique souvenir, the Spice Market is a sensory delight for the palate and the senses.

Le Marché aux Epices, Basse-Terre:
For an authentic taste of local life, venture to Le Marché aux Epices in Basse-Terre. This bustling market is a treasure trove of fresh produce, local delicacies, and handmade crafts. From tropical fruits and spices to handwoven baskets and Madras fabric, the market reflects the everyday vibrancy of Guadeloupean culture. Immerse yourself in the lively exchanges between vendors and locals, discovering the genuine warmth that defines the island.

Shopping Districts in Le Gosier:
Indulge in a shopping spree in the vibrant districts of Le Gosier, where boutique shops and local markets offer an eclectic array of goods. From stylish resort wear to authentic Madras accessories, these shopping districts provide a mix of contemporary fashion and traditional crafts. Uncover unique souvenirs that capture the essence of Guadeloupe's style and cultural heritage.

Guadeloupe's markets and shopping districts are not just about acquiring goods; they're about immersing yourself in the lively pulse of the island. Whether you're strolling through craft markets, savoring the scents of spices, or indulging in a shopping spree, each experience is a vibrant chapter in your Guadeloupean adventure, a chance to bring home the authentic spirit of the Caribbean.

CHAPTER 7: 7-DAY ITINERARY IN GUADELOUPE

Day 1: A Warm Guadeloupean Welcome

Morning: Arrival at Pointe-à-Pitre International Airport
As the plane descends over turquoise waters, you catch the first glimpses of Guadeloupe's lush landscapes. Touch down at Pointe-à-Pitre International Airport, your gateway to this Caribbean haven. The warm breeze welcomes you, and the anticipation of a week filled with adventure begins.

Afternoon: Explore Pointe-à-Pitre's Charm
Head to your chosen accommodation to drop off your bags and freshen up. For the afternoon, dive into the heart of Guadeloupe's urban charm by exploring Pointe-à-Pitre. Begin at Place de la Victoire, where colonial architecture and vibrant markets blend seamlessly. Wander through the spice-scented stalls of the Spice Market, immersing yourself in the island's flavors. Stop for a traditional Creole lunch at a local eatery, savoring the fusion of French and Caribbean cuisines.

Evening: Sunset by La Darse Marina
As evening approaches, make your way to La Darse Marina, a picturesque harbor in Pointe-à-Pitre. The setting sun casts a warm glow over the sailboats and waterside cafes. Relax with a leisurely dinner at one of the waterfront restaurants, indulging in fresh seafood and Creole specialties. Let the evening unfold with a stroll along the marina, absorbing the lively atmosphere and the

vibrant colors of the sunset. Your first day in Guadeloupe culminates with the promise of the adventures that lie ahead.

Day 2: Basse-Terre's Natural Wonders

Morning: Discover the Soufrière Volcano
Begin your day early and head to Basse-Terre to explore the iconic La Soufrière Volcano. The winding road through lush rainforests takes you to the trailhead. Embark on the Chemin des Dames trail, surrounded by the sounds of exotic birds and the scent of tropical flora. The trail leads to breathtaking viewpoints, offering panoramic vistas of the Caribbean Sea. Reaching the summit, stand in awe of the volcanic landscapes and the island's beauty spread out below.

Afternoon: Lunch in Deshaies and Visit to Jardin Botanique
Descend from the volcano and journey to Deshaies for a well-deserved lunch in this charming seaside town. Enjoy a meal at a local restaurant, savoring the flavors of Guadeloupean cuisine. Post-lunch, explore the Jardin Botanique de Deshaies, a botanical garden created by the renowned French comedian Coluche. Wander through lush pathways surrounded by vibrant flora and encounter exotic plant species from around the world.

Evening: Relax on Grande-Anse Beach
Conclude your day with a visit to Grande-Anse Beach, one of Basse-Terre's stunning coastal gems. The golden sand stretches along the azure waters, creating a perfect setting for relaxation. Whether you choose to dip your toes in the warm Caribbean Sea or simply unwind on the shore, Grande-Anse provides a serene ambiance as the sun sets. Wrap up your day with a seaside dinner at a local beachfront restaurant, enjoying the tranquil sounds of the waves..

Day 3: Les Saintes Archipelago Expedition

Morning: Ferry to Terre-de-Haut
Embark on an early morning ferry from Trois-Rivières to the enchanting Les Saintes archipelago. Arrive at Terre-de-Haut and start your day with a stroll through the charming village. Visit Fort Napoléon des Saintes, perched on a hill, for panoramic views of the archipelago. Engage with the island's history through the museum within the fort.

Afternoon: Secluded Bliss at Anse Crawen
For a tranquil afternoon, head to Anse Crawen, a secluded beach surrounded by nature's tranquility. The clear waters and powdery sand provide an ideal spot for swimming or simply basking in the serenity. Enjoy a beachside picnic with local treats and relish the unhurried pace of Les Saintes.

Evening: Sunset and Local Cuisine
As the day winds down, find a seaside restaurant to witness the sunset over the Caribbean Sea. Indulge in a delightful dinner, savoring the freshness of seafood and Creole specialties. The starlit sky above Les Saintes adds a magical touch to your evening.

Day 4: Guadeloupe National Park Adventure

Morning: Explore La Grande Vigie and Anse du Souffleur
Return to Basse-Terre and begin your morning at La Grande Vigie. This dramatic cliff offers panoramic views of the Atlantic

Ocean and the lush landscapes below. Continue to Anse du Souffleur, a secluded beach known for its calm waters. Take a refreshing swim and enjoy the tranquility of this hidden gem.

Afternoon: Hike in Guadeloupe National Park
After a beachside lunch, venture into Guadeloupe National Park. Choose a hiking trail that suits your preferences, whether it's the challenging Parcours de la Soufrière or a leisurely walk through the forest. Immerse yourself in the park's biodiversity, encountering waterfalls, exotic plants, and the captivating Carbet Falls.

Evening: Local Dinner in Saint-Claude
Head to Saint-Claude for an authentic Creole dinner at a local eatery. The town's elevated location provides a cooler climate, and the culinary offerings showcase the diverse flavors of Guadeloupean cuisine. Reflect on the day's adventures as you savor the local delicacies.

Day 5: Cultural Exploration in Saint-François

Morning: Visit Saint-François Market and Marina
Travel to Saint-François on Grande-Terre and start your morning at the lively Saint-François Market. Explore stalls filled with fresh produce, spices, and handmade crafts. Stroll along the marina, admiring the boats and absorbing the coastal ambiance.

Afternoon: Relax at Plage de la Caravelle
Spend your afternoon at Plage de la Caravelle, a picturesque beach with golden sands. Engage in water sports like windsurfing

or simply unwind under the Caribbean sun. Enjoy a beachfront lunch at one of the local eateries, savoring the flavors of the sea.

Evening: Sunset at Pointe des Châteaux
Head to Pointe des Châteaux for a breathtaking sunset experience. This rugged peninsula offers panoramic views of the Atlantic Ocean. Capture the changing hues of the sky as the sun dips below the horizon. Conclude your day with a seaside dinner in Saint-François, celebrating the beauty of the Caribbean night.

Day 6: Culinary Delights in Sainte-Anne

Morning: Relax at Plage de la Perle
Begin your day with a visit to Plage de la Perle near Deshaies. This unique black-sand beach provides a serene setting for a morning of relaxation. Take a leisurely swim or stroll along the shoreline, appreciating the distinct beauty of this coastal haven.

Afternoon: Culinary Adventure at Marché de Sainte-Anne
Explore the vibrant Marché de Sainte-Anne, where a culinary adventure awaits. Sample local dishes, tropical fruits, and Creole specialties from the market stalls. Engage with the vendors to learn about the island's culinary traditions and flavors.

Evening: Sunset at Le Ti'Punch Bar
As the sun sets, make your way to Le Ti'Punch Bar for a relaxed evening. Sip on traditional island elixirs and enjoy the laid-back ambiance. The bar often hosts live music or cultural events, providing a perfect blend of entertainment and relaxation.

Day 7: Farewell to Guadeloupe

Morning: Final Beachside Moments
Savor your last morning in Guadeloupe with a visit to a favorite beach or a seaside spot of your choosing. Whether it's revisiting a beloved beach or discovering a new one, relish the tranquility and beauty of the Caribbean shores.

Afternoon: Souvenir Shopping in Le Gosier
Head to the vibrant shopping districts in Le Gosier for some souvenir shopping. Explore boutique shops offering unique items, local crafts, and stylish finds. Purchase mementos that capture the essence of your Guadeloupean journey.

Evening: Farewell Dinner in Le Gosier
Conclude your week with a farewell dinner in Le Gosier. Choose a restaurant overlooking the marina or one with live music for a festive atmosphere. Relish the flavors of Creole cuisine and toast to the memories created during your unforgettable week in Guadeloupe.

This seven-day itinerary is designed to offer a diverse and immersive experience, allowing you to discover the natural beauty, cultural richness, and culinary delights of Guadeloupe. Adjustments can be made based on personal preferences and interests.

CHAPTER 8: PRACTICAL INFORMATION AND TIPS

Etiquette and Customs

In Guadeloupe, etiquette and customs are woven into the fabric of daily life, reflecting the warmth and respect inherent in Caribbean culture. As a visitor, embracing these customs enhances your experience and fosters meaningful connections with the locals.

Greeting with a Warm Smile:
The essence of Guadeloupean hospitality begins with a genuine smile. Whether meeting someone for the first time or entering a local establishment, a warm and friendly greeting sets a positive tone. It's customary to offer a friendly "Bonjour" (good morning) or "Bonsoir" (good evening) as you navigate the island's diverse spaces.

Respecting Personal Space:
Guadeloupeans value personal space and maintain a relaxed approach to time. While interactions are warm and engaging, it's essential to respect the unhurried pace of conversations. Take the time to connect, listen, and share stories, allowing relationships to unfold naturally.

Dress Code: Casual Elegance:
The dress code in Guadeloupe leans towards casual elegance. Whether exploring vibrant markets, dining at local eateries, or enjoying the beaches, comfortable and stylish attire is suitable. If planning to attend a religious site or upscale restaurant, slightly more formal clothing is appreciated.

Language: Embracing Creole and French:
While French is the official language, Guadeloupean Creole (Kréyòl) is a vibrant expression of the local identity. Locals appreciate visitors making an effort to embrace both languages, even if only with basic greetings. A simple "Bonjour" or "Bonsoir" in Creole resonates warmly with the community.

Dining Etiquette: Savoring the Culinary Experience:
Mealtime in Guadeloupe is a celebration, and dining etiquette reflects the island's rich culinary traditions. It's customary to savor each bite and engage in unhurried conversations during meals. When dining in a local's home, it's a gracious gesture to express appreciation for the delicious fare.

Cultural Sensitivity: Honoring Traditions:
Guadeloupeans take pride in their cultural heritage, which is deeply intertwined with African, European, and Caribbean influences. Demonstrating cultural sensitivity involves appreciating and respecting local traditions, whether it's participating in a Gwoka dance or attending a traditional festival. Engaging with the island's history fosters a deeper understanding of its people.

Tipping and Service: An Appreciative Gesture:
Tipping is generally practiced in Guadeloupe, and it's considered an appreciative gesture for good service. In restaurants, rounding up the bill or leaving a 5-10% tip is customary. Additionally, expressing gratitude with a simple "merci" (thank you) goes a long way in acknowledging the efforts of those who contribute to your experience.

Embracing the etiquette and customs of Guadeloupe adds a layer of authenticity to your journey. As you navigate the island's cultural nuances with an open heart and respect, you'll find yourself not just a visitor but a welcomed participant in the vibrant tapestry of Guadeloupean life.

Language and Communication

In Guadeloupe, language is a mosaic, a colorful blend of French and Creole that reflects the island's diverse cultural heritage. Understanding the nuances of language and communication opens a gateway to authentic connections and a deeper appreciation of the local way of life.

French, the Official Language:
French serves as the official language of Guadeloupe, used in government, education, and formal settings. While many locals are fluent in French, especially in urban areas, there is a warm appreciation when visitors make an effort to converse in the official language. Simple phrases such as "Bonjour" (good morning), "Merci" (thank you), and "Au revoir" (goodbye) go a long way in fostering positive interactions.

Creole, the Heartbeat of Communication:
Guadeloupean Creole, often referred to as Kréyòl, is the soulful heartbeat of communication among the locals. This rich and expressive language has deep roots in the history of the Caribbean and is infused with African, European, and indigenous influences. While French is used in formal settings, Creole is the language of daily life, infused with a warmth and rhythm that resonates with the island's spirit.

Navigating Bilingual Conversations:
In Guadeloupe, it's common to experience bilingual conversations seamlessly shifting between French and Creole. Locals appreciate visitors who embrace this linguistic dance, and a willingness to engage in both languages enhances the depth of your cultural experience. Don't hesitate to ask for help or

clarification in either French or Creole, as Guadeloupeans are generally eager to assist.

Language of the Streets: Creole's Everyday Presence:
As you explore the markets, streets, and local neighborhoods, you'll find Creole as the language of the streets. Street vendors, musicians, and locals engaged in everyday conversations often express themselves in the lyrical cadence of Creole. Take a moment to soak in the sounds, appreciate the vibrancy, and perhaps pick up a few common Creole expressions along the way.

Learning a Few Creole Phrases:
While many Guadeloupeans are bilingual, learning a few Creole phrases adds a personal touch to your interactions. A friendly "Sa ka maché?" (How are you?), "Mwen renmen sa" (I like that), or "An nou alé" (Let's go) can create smiles and foster a sense of camaraderie.

Cultural Understanding through Language:
Language is a key to unlocking the cultural treasures of Guadeloupe. As you engage with locals in their linguistic tapestry, you gain not just words but a deeper understanding of the island's history, traditions, and the resilient spirit of its people. Embrace the multilingual symphony, and let the language of Guadeloupe become a bridge to heartfelt connections and shared moments.

Simple French Phrases to Know

Greetings and Politeness:
Bonjour - Good morning (bohn-zhoor)
Bonsoir - Good evening (bohn-swahr)
Merci - Thank you (mehr-see)
S'il vous plaît - Please (seel voo pleh)
Excusez-moi - Excuse me (ehk-skew-zay mwah)

Common Expressions:
Oui - Yes (wee)
Non - No (noh)
D'accord - Okay (dah-kor)
Bien sûr - Of course (byen soor)
Pas de problème - No problem (pah duh proh-blehm)

Basic Conversational Phrases:
Comment ça va? - How are you? (koh-mahn sah vah)
Je ne comprends pas - I don't understand (zhuh nuh kohm-prahn pah)
Parlez-vous anglais? - Do you speak English? (par-lei voo ahn-glay)
Pouvez-vous m'aider? - Can you help me? (poo-veh voo mey-dey)

Navigating the City:
Où est... ? - Where is...? (oo eh)
La rue principale - Main street (lah roo pran-si-pal)
La station de métro - Metro station (lah stah-syon duh may-tro)
L'office de tourisme - Tourist office (lo-fees duh too-ris-muh)

Dining Out:
La carte, s'il vous plaît - The menu, please (lah kart, seel voo pleh)

L'addition, s'il vous plaît - The bill, please (la-dee-syon, seel voo pleh)
Une table pour deux, s'il vous plaît - A table for two, please (ewn tahbl poor du, seel voo pleh)
C'est délicieux - It's delicious (say day-lee-syu)

Shopping:
Combien ça coûte? - How much does it cost? (kohm-byen sah koot)
Puis-je payer avec une carte? - Can I pay with a card? (pwee-jei pei-ay ah-vek ewn kart)
Avez-vous ceci en d'autres couleurs? - Do you have this in other colors? (ah-vey voo suh ahn do-tr koo-luhr)

Emergency Phrases:
Aidez-moi! - Help me! (eh-dey mwah)
J'ai besoin d'aide - I need help (zhay buh-zwahn dayd)
Où est l'hôpital le plus proche? - Where is the nearest hospital? (oo eh lo-pee-tal luh ploo prosh)

Remember, confidence matters more than perfection when using a new language. Feel free to embrace these phrases, and don't hesitate to ask locals for help or clarification—your efforts will be appreciated. Bon voyage!

Health and Safety Tips for Your Guadeloupe Adventure

Embarking on a journey to Guadeloupe promises a tapestry of experiences, and ensuring your well-being enhances every moment. Here are essential health and safety tips to make your trip a worry-free exploration:

1. Stay Hydrated:
The Caribbean sun can be intense, so it's crucial to stay hydrated. Carry a reusable water bottle and sip water regularly, especially during outdoor activities. Coconut water, readily available on the island, is a refreshing and natural electrolyte boost.

2. Sun Protection:
Guadeloupe enjoys a tropical climate, and sun protection is paramount. Pack and apply sunscreen with a high SPF, wear a wide-brimmed hat, and use sunglasses to shield your eyes from the sun's rays. Reapply sunscreen, especially if you're engaging in water activities.

3. Mosquito Protection:
While Guadeloupe is generally mosquito-friendly, it's wise to protect yourself from potential bites. Use insect repellent, especially during the evening and in forested areas. Consider wearing long sleeves and pants, particularly if venturing into the rainforest.

4. Medical Precautions:
Ensure your routine vaccinations are up to date. While no specific vaccinations are mandatory for Guadeloupe, it's advisable to consult with your healthcare provider for personalized

recommendations. Carry a basic first aid kit with essentials like bandages, antiseptic, and any necessary personal medications.

5. Water Safety:
Guadeloupe boasts pristine beaches and inviting waters. While enjoying the sea, adhere to safety guidelines. Choose beaches with lifeguards, swim in designated areas, and pay attention to warning flags. If you're unfamiliar with local conditions, inquire with locals or authorities for advice.

6. Local Cuisine Caution:
Sampling Guadeloupe's diverse cuisine is a must, but exercise caution with street food to prevent foodborne illnesses. Opt for freshly prepared items and ensure that seafood is cooked thoroughly. Drink bottled or treated water and avoid consuming raw or undercooked dishes.

7. Respect Nature:
Guadeloupe is renowned for its lush landscapes and biodiversity. Respect nature by staying on designated trails during hikes, avoiding the disturbance of wildlife, and refraining from littering. Adhering to eco-friendly practices contributes to the preservation of the island's natural beauty.

8. Transportation Safety:
Whether renting a car or using public transportation, prioritize safety. Follow local traffic rules, wear seatbelts, and exercise caution on winding roads. If using scooters or bicycles, wear helmets and exercise vigilance, especially in high-traffic areas.

9. Emergency Services Awareness:
Familiarize yourself with local emergency contact numbers and the location of medical facilities. In case of an emergency, the

universal emergency number is 112. Additionally, carry essential information such as your accommodation's address and contact details.

10. Hygienic Practices:
Maintain good hygiene practices by washing hands regularly, especially before meals. Carry hand sanitizer for situations where handwashing facilities may be limited. Be mindful of your surroundings and maintain a clean and organized personal space.

By incorporating these health and safety tips into your travel routine, you'll not only safeguard your well-being but also create the ideal conditions for an enriching and enjoyable exploration of Guadeloupe's treasures. Safe travels!

Emergency Contacts

In case of any emergency during your visit to Guadeloupe, it's essential to be aware of the local contact numbers and services. Here are the primary emergency contacts you should know:

1. General Emergency Services:
Emergency Number: 112 (This is the universal emergency number)

2. Medical Emergencies:
Ambulance and Medical Assistance: 15

3. Police and Law Enforcement:
Police Emergency: 17

4. Fire Department:
Fire Emergency: 18

5. Tourist Police:
Tourist Police (Pointe-à-Pitre): +590 590 82 57 89
Tourist Police (Saint-François): +590 590 88 49 49

6. Search and Rescue (at Sea):
Maritime Gendarmerie: +590 590 93 30 17

7. Poison Control:
Poison Control Center: +33 1 40 05 48 48

8. Consular Assistance:
Embassy of your country in France: Contact information can be obtained from your embassy or consulate before travel.

When calling emergency services, it's advisable to have a basic understanding of French or Creole. However, English may be understood in tourist-centric areas.

Keep a copy of your passport and important documents in a secure location.

If you require consular assistance, contact the embassy or consulate of your country.

Ensure that you have these numbers saved and easily accessible during your stay in Guadeloupe. In case of an emergency, don't hesitate to reach out to the appropriate services for assistance. Your safety is a priority, and being prepared adds an extra layer of security to your travel experience.

Communication and Internet Access in Guadeloupe

When it comes to staying connected in Guadeloupe, the island offers a blend of modern communication facilities and the laid-back charm of the Caribbean lifestyle.

Mobile Networks:
Guadeloupe is well-covered by mobile networks, ensuring that you can stay connected throughout your journey. Major local carriers provide reliable service across the main islands, offering voice, text, and data services. Check with your home mobile provider regarding international roaming options and charges or consider purchasing a local SIM card for the duration of your stay.

Internet Access:
Most accommodations, including hotels, resorts, and vacation rentals, provide internet access for guests. Additionally, cafes, restaurants, and public spaces often offer free Wi-Fi. In urban areas like Pointe-à-Pitre and Saint-François, you'll find internet cafés and co-working spaces for more extended connectivity needs.

Public Wi-Fi:
Public places such as airports, shopping centers, and tourist attractions may have free Wi-Fi hotspots. While these can be convenient for quick tasks, it's advisable to use secure connections for sensitive activities.

Local SIM Cards:

For a more cost-effective and data-centric approach, consider purchasing a local SIM card upon arrival. This option allows you to enjoy local rates for calls, texts, and data. SIM cards are available at major airports, shopping centers, and local mobile providers.

Language of Communication:
While French is the official language, many locals in tourist areas understand and speak English. However, outside these areas, especially in smaller towns and rural regions, proficiency in French or basic Creole phrases can be immensely helpful for effective communication.

Postal Services:
If you need to send postcards or letters, Guadeloupe has efficient postal services. Post offices, known as "La Poste," can be found in major towns. Keep in mind that international mail may take some time, so plan accordingly.

Emergency Communications:
In case of emergencies, the universal emergency number, 112, can be dialed for assistance. Save this number in your contacts for quick access.

Satellite Phones:
If you plan to explore more remote areas or engage in outdoor adventures, having a satellite phone could be beneficial, as connectivity may vary in certain regions.

Navigating with Apps:
Popular navigation apps work well in Guadeloupe, aiding in exploring the islands and finding local attractions. Download

offline maps to ensure functionality even in areas with limited connectivity.

Guadeloupe offers a delightful blend of modern connectivity and the unhurried pace of island life. Whether you're sharing your travel experiences online or simply staying in touch with loved ones, the communication infrastructure in Guadeloupe ensures you can do so seamlessly.

Useful Apps, Websites, and Maps

Navigating Guadeloupe's treasures is made easier with a selection of handy apps, informative websites, and reliable maps designed to enhance your travel experience.

1. Maps.me:
For offline navigation, Maps.me is a traveler's ally. Download the Guadeloupe map in advance, and you'll have access to detailed maps, points of interest, and hiking trails without the need for a constant internet connection. Find it at [www.maps.me]

2. Waze:
Waze is an excellent real-time navigation app that provides up-to-date traffic information, optimal routes, and road conditions. It's particularly handy for exploring Guadeloupe's scenic landscapes. Download it at [www.waze.com]

3. Guadeloupe Islands Tourist Board Website:
The official website of the Guadeloupe Islands Tourist Board is a valuable resource for trip planning. Discover comprehensive information on attractions, events, accommodations, and more at [www.guadeloupe-islands.com]

4. Airbnb:
If you prefer unique accommodations, Airbnb lists a variety of options across Guadeloupe. Immerse yourself in the local culture by staying in charming apartments, villas, or cottages. Explore offerings at [www.airbnb.com]

5. TripAdvisor:
TripAdvisor remains a reliable source for traveler reviews, recommendations, and insights. Discover top-rated restaurants,

attractions, and hidden gems based on fellow travelers' experiences. Visit [www.tripadvisor.com]

6. Booking.com:
Booking.com offers a diverse range of accommodations, from luxury resorts to budget-friendly stays. Secure your ideal lodging by exploring options at [www.booking.com]

7. Le Routard Guidebook:
While not a digital app, the "Le Routard" guidebook is a popular French travel guide series. Look for the Guadeloupe edition for insightful tips, cultural information, and local recommendations.

8. Gwoka:
Immerse yourself in Guadeloupe's rich musical tradition with the Gwoka app. Gwoka is not just music; it's a cultural experience. Learn more at [www.gwokamusics.com]

9. French Phrases - Lonely Planet:
Enhance your communication with locals by learning basic French phrases using the Lonely Planet French Phrasebook app. Find it on [www.lonelyplanet.com]

10. Google Translate:
Overcome language barriers with Google Translate. Download language packs for offline use, allowing you to translate text or speech without an internet connection. Access it at [translate.google.com]

Whether you're exploring hiking trails, finding the perfect beach, or seeking local insights, these apps, websites, and maps will be valuable companions on your Guadeloupean journey. Bon voyage!

CONCLUSION

As we come to the end of this Guadeloupe travel guide, I hope you've felt the rhythm of this Caribbean gem, heard the laughter echoing on its beaches, and tasted the vibrant flavors that make up its culinary mosaic. Guadeloupe, with its lush landscapes and warm-hearted locals, is more than just a destination—it's an experience painted with the colors of adventure, relaxation, and cultural richness.

As you've navigated through the chapters, envisioning the turquoise waters of Grande-Anse and the vibrant markets of Sainte-Anne, I trust you've unearthed the essence of this tropical haven. Guadeloupe invites you to dance to the beat of its music, explore the trails of La Soufrière, and savor each moment under the Caribbean sun.

The journey is not just about the landmarks and attractions; it's about the connections made, the stories heard, and the flavors savored. From the historic streets of Pointe-à-Pitre to the serene beauty of Les Saintes, Guadeloupe unfolds its wonders with a warmth that lingers in the heart.

As you plan your adventure, consider the practical tips, immerse yourself in the local culture, and let the spirit of Guadeloupe guide your steps. Whether you're seeking the thrill of outdoor adventures, the tranquility of secluded beaches, or the vibrancy of local festivals, Guadeloupe is ready to offer a palette of experiences.

So, my fellow traveler, get ready to embark on a journey that transcends the pages of this guide. Let the allure of Guadeloupe beckon you, and may your footsteps echo with the laughter of newfound friends and the rustle of palm leaves in the breeze. Whether you're a solo explorer, a couple seeking romance, or a family in search of unforgettable moments, Guadeloupe welcomes you with open arms and a promise of unparalleled Caribbean magic.

As you pack your bags and prepare for the adventure ahead, remember that the real beauty of Guadeloupe lies not just in its picturesque landscapes but in the memories you'll create. So, set your compass for this captivating Caribbean jewel, and let Guadeloupe be the backdrop to your next unforgettable chapter. Bon voyage!

Printed in Great Britain
by Amazon